The Commissioner's Corner

Steve —

It was great to
work with you at HPG this
April (2008). Thanks for everything
you do for learning.

[signature]

The Commissioner's Corner

F. Darnall Daley, Jr.

2007

The Commissioner's Corner

Contents

This volume is dedicated to the hundreds and hundreds of men and women that I have worked with over the years who devote a large part of their lives to the youth of our world wide community through Scouting. It is dedicated especially to my friends Dick Bennett and Dave Horton who have been my inspiration in Scouting. And finally I dedicate it to my wife, Ernie, who I met at dancing class in September 1950. I hope she will always save the last dance for me.

Foreword

When I became the Council Executive of the Hawk Mountain Council in 1988 Darnall Daley was already the Council Commissioner and was already inspiring the Scouts and Scouters in our council with these monthly essays under a mast head of "The Commissioner's Corner." I have often remarked that if you called central casting for someone to play the part of the Council Commissioner, the person you would get would be someone who looked and acted much like Darnall. Darnall has the ability to inspire volunteers and to energize the program. In these pages you will find a selection of the inspirational paragraphs that we published in the *Herbie Hawk News* over the 16 years that he was our Council Commissioner. Darnall has the ability to convey to you his deep understanding of the true meaning of Scouting. His sincerity and passion for the Scouting movement comes through in all of these essays. He presents here little nuggets of wisdom on how to run Scouting units. He brings to the front a sense of perspective on what is important in the Scouting movement. I hope that you will enjoy these stories as much as I have.

Yours in Scouting,

Richard C. Bennett
Scout Executive
Hawk Mountain Council
December 2006

Author's Note: Dick Bennett was my friend and inspiration in Scouting for almost 20 years. Dick retired as Scout Executive of the Hawk Mountain Council at the end of February 2007. We all were saddened when he passed away in May 2007.

Introduction

My Scouting career as a youth was suddenly and dramatically ended when one Sunday my mother ordered me to get into the family car. I shortly there after found myself ensconced in a military boarding school no doubt as a reward for my good behavior. I was twelve at the time. I had been a Cub Scout in Pack 35 and then a Tenderfoot Scout in Troop 35 in the Baltimore Area Council.

My adult Scouting involvement started when I went to pick up my son at a Troop meeting. The old Scoutmaster asked me to hang around and help out. That first Troop meeting was 37 years ago. In the years since then I have served as an Assistant Scoutmaster and then as Scoutmaster for Troop 423 in the Baltimore Area Council; as Assistant District Commissioner, District Commissioner, and then as an Assistant Scoutmaster of Troop 101 Marshfield in the Old Colony Council. In the Hawk Mountain Council I've served as an Assistant Council Commissioner, Council Vice President for Relationships, and for the a period of 16 years as Council Commissioner. In the last few years I have also been an Assistant Cubmaster in Pack 431 with one grandson and Assistant Scoutmaster in Troop 431 that included another grandson.

In Scouting they never really let you get away. Within minutes of deciding that I would not seek reelection as Council Commissioner I was approached to serve as Area Vice President—Commissioner Service. (Well, OK, it wasn't minutes, it just seemed that way.) More recently I agreed after some major arm twisting to be the host for our monthly local TV show called "The Scouting Perspective." If you'd like more detail about my Scouting background you could check out my website (www.DarnallDaley.com).

Over the years that I was the Council Commissioner of the Hawk Mount Council I wrote a short essay each month for the Hawk Mountain Council's *Herbie Hawk News*. In the end there were 144 of these essays and 41,000 words. This book is a collection of some of those essays. I hope that I've cut out the ones that are no longer of interest.

I want to take this opportunity to thank all of you that have helped with the success we have enjoyed in the Hawk Mountain Council in the years that I have served as your commissioner. I hope that you are as inspired by the rereading of these little stories as I was by you during the years that I was your Council Commissioner. I'd also like to thank Brian Quinter of Stardust Photographic Studio for taking the cover pictures.

F. Darnall Daley, Jr.
Wyomissing, PA
fdarnall@comcast.net
www.TheCommissionersCorner.com
November 2007

The Early Years—1986-1989

Roundtables

Do you need just one more idea for your Unit's program? Are you having a couple of problems that you'd like to discuss with more experienced Unit leaders? The place where both of these and many other things happen is at the District Roundtable each month. Roundtables are a training experience designed to help you with your Unit's program. Roundtables are a fellowship opportunity designed to demonstrate that you're not "alone" doing your job in Scouting.

Scouting is the finest program available to youth today. Make sure your kids get the most out of it by making sure you take advantage of every training experience available to you!

Ask your Unit Commissioner to take you to the next Roundtable in your District. [*Herbie Hawk News*, November, 1986]

Scout Week

Does your church charter a Scout unit? If so, now is the time for you to be planning for the celebration of Scout Week.

During February each year we celebrate our anniversary.

This year [1987] Scout week will start with Scout Sunday on February 8th and end with Scout Sabbath on February 14th.

Please take advantage of this anniversary by arranging with the leaders of your Cub Pack or Scout Troop and the leaders of your church to have some kind of special program to celebrate Scout Sunday/Scout Sabbath. This is a good opportunity for the members of your church to renew their commitment to Scouting and for the members of your Scout unit to demonstrate that "A Scout is reverent."

Boy Scouts and Cub Scouts can be used during the service as ushers, acolytes, and as readers, Scout Sunday/ Scout Sabbath is a good time to make the unit charter presentation. Youth and adult religious awards can be presented during these services.

Please call your unit commissioner if you need any help with this. [*Herbie Hawk News*, December, 1986]

Advancement

How is the advancement record in your Unit? Is every boy in your Unit advancing at least one badge or rank each year?

One of the most important Scouting methods is the recognition that our boys receive through the advancement program.

When a boy earns a badge, he has not only progressed at his own pace, but we get an opportunity to recognize this advancement. If you think that the boys don't enjoy this, then take a good look at their faces the next time you hand out an award. The self esteem that advancement builds is one of the items that keep boys in Scouting.

Take a look at the advancement program in your Unit. If it's not up to what you would like, give your Unit

Commissioner a call. Ask him/her to help you establish a more active advancement program. If you can't get in touch with your Unit Commissioner, please call your District Commissioner whose phone number can be found elsewhere in this paper.

Remember you can't recognize a boy too many times for each award. [*Herbie Hawk News*, February, 1987]

Good Turns

It was a good turn done for William D. Boyce in the 1909 London fog by an unknown British Boy Scout that brought Scouting to the United States. [We now know, of course, that the story of the boy in the London fog was a story made up by James E West.] Doing good turns through community service and helping others is not only our motto but it plays a big part in the values that we want our young people to understand and it is part of the Scouting method. It is important that our Cub Scouts and Boy Scouts come to understand the joy that sharing of ourselves can bring.

This year Scouting is participating in three National Good Turns. The first is the donor Awareness Program—a program that we've undertaken at the request of President Reagan. Second is the Child Abuse Awareness Program and the third is the Drug Awareness, which you will be reading about in this month's *Scouter Magazine* and in **Boys' Life**. A fourth good turn a Council-wide food collection that we will undertake in the spring.

If your Unit participates in these Good Turns and all the others that you usually do, we will really have a positive impact on all the youth in our community, in and out of

Scouting. Therefore, I hope that you will make sure that your Unit is an active participant in these projects.

Please call your Unit Commissioner, if you need any additional information or help with this. [*Herbie Hawk News*, March, 1987]

Summer Camp

I would hope that by now your Cub Pack is signed up for Day Camp and that your Scout Troop is signed up for Summer Camp. If not, please take care of this as soon as possible.

After your Unit is signed up to go, the next thing is to make sure that all your boys are going to go with you. Like everything else in our busy lives today, if you want to have a good turn out, then you'll have to take time to promote the event.

Show slides of your Unit at Camp at your next Pack or Troop Meeting. Show slides after a church service to the parents and to the boys. Get your District Camping Committee to come in and put on their program. Send cards and letters to the families. Hold Family Meetings for everyone associates with your Unit. In short, do everything that you can think of to PROMOTE Summer Camp for your Unit and every boy in it.

If money will be a problem for some or all of your boys, then start the money earning projects now. I cannot imagine a richer experience for any boy than a week a camp for which he has earned the money himself.

Please call your Unit Commissioner, if you need any additional information or help with this. [*Herbie Hawk News*, April, 1987]

Recruiting Parents

Are you having trouble getting enough of the parents of the boys in your Unit to help? Of course you are; all Units have this problem.

I can't help but think that when this is the case, we haven't explained to these parents how important Scouting is. They equate Scouting with karate class and trombone lessons. If we're really able to explain how important Scouting is to their sons, they'd be there to help us.

Next time you're trying to recruit the parents of one of your Cubs or Scouts to help with your unit, think of all the reasons that you're involved and all of the reasons that you like to see your sons active in Scouting. Use these reasons to explain how important you feel your Scouting work is and just maybe you'll get the help you want. [*Herbie Hawk News*, May, 1987]

Is Your Unit's Program Fun?

We often talk about why the Scouting program is important and discuss why we are involved in Scouting.

What I'd like you to think about today is why our young people are so interested in being a part of Scouting. I suspect that you will reach the conclusion that their reason is quite different from ours. We would like to do our part in shaping the leaders of tomorrow. No nine year old, on the other hand, has any interest in this. Our nine year old gets enough of preparing for tomorrow in school.

What our young people want is a program that is fun. For our Cub Scout this means a program that includes games, songs, skits, crafts, and all the other activities that are listed in the program guides and that are discussed each month at the Roundtables.

For Boy Scouts this means running a Troop by the Scouting method and letting the boy leaders decide what activity THEY think is fun.

Make sure that your unit's program is fun and you'll have a strong program that will attract the youth of your community year, after year, after year. [*Herbie Hawk News*, October, 1987]

Scout Leader Training

I THINK YOU SHOULD DEMAND YOUR RIGHTS!

Every leader in Scouting is entitled to be trained in their Scouting job. It's your right to be trained and you should stick up for your rights. Not only will you benefit but the youth in your unit will benefit.

If you're a new leader, Fast Start Training is available. Make sure that you get it.

If you are a Cub Scout Leader, Cub Scout Leader training is held in every district every year. Demand your rights.

If you are a Boy Scout Leader, you should attend Boy Scout leader training.

The Roundtables held in your District every month can often be the best training experience of all. Make sure you get some.

In addition there are many, many other training opportunities. Remember training equals knowledge and knowledge equals a quality program. So demand your rights. Get trained, not only for your sake but for the sake of the youth in your unit and all of the young people in our community. [*Herbie Hawk News*, November, 1987]

Advancement Trail

Advancement is an important part of the Scouting Program and the purpose of the advancement is to help our boys grow. I want to point this out because some of you seem to have another idea.

The idea is to recognize each and every step that a boy takes along the advancement trail. I had the honor recently to present the Eagle Badge to one of our Scouts. This award was made, as it should have been, with great pomp and ceremony.

We should remember, though, the Eagle Scout is the last step in the advancement process, not our goal. For boys who earn the Wolf Badge, Second Class, a Merit Badge, or even a Skill Award, the accomplishment at that time may be just as great as for the same boy when he later earns Eagle. [Do you remember Skill Awards? Reference to Skill Awards makes this essay a little dated but I'm sure you get the idea.] Advancement is designed to recognize a boy for accomplishing what he is able to accomplish at this moment in time.

So recognize your Cubs and Boy Scouts for each and every advancement in every way that you can think of. Make announcements at Pack or Troop meetings. Hold a Court of Honor. Have a short ceremony in church on Scout Sunday. Do all three. Don't pass up any opportunity to let the world know what your boys have done.

Please call your Unit Commissioner or your District Commissioner, if you need any help with this. [*Herbie Hawk News*, December, 1987]

Scout Week

Each year in February we celebrate Scout Week.

If your church charters a Scouting Unit, either a Troop or a Cub Pack, this week is a good time to hold Scout Sunday. You can invite the entire Scout Troop and/or Cub Pack to attend a Sunday Service, in uniform, and to serve as ushers, acolytes, and as lay readers.

During the service it would be appropriate to present Scout Awards, youth religious awards, or to have a charter presentation ceremony.

Inviting your Scout Troop or Cub Pack to church on Scout Sunday will accomplish a number of things. First of all, inviting them will extend the outreach of your church to all of your Scouts. Second, you will remind your congregation that this is their Scout Unit. Next, you will get the opportunity to recognize the accomplishments of your Cubs and Scouts. Finally, Scout Sunday can be a wonderful and moving experience for you, for the Scouts, for the Scout Leaders, and for the congregation. [*Herbie Hawk News*, January, 1988]

Hazing

It has come to my attention that some Scout Troops still permit the hazing of new Scouts.

Older Scouts sometimes feel that new Scouts should be "initiated" into the troop with a hazing activity. Sometimes this takes the form of trying to scare Cub Scouts and other potential recruits.

The overall effect of these activities is that you lose boys from your program and you don't get boys into your Unit that would otherwise have an opportunity to benefit from the Scouting program. In addition young boys that we are trying to help to manhood get mistreated.

I hope that you will agree with me that hazing has no place in Scouting. Please be alert to this desire of older boys to haze the new Scouts and direct their efforts into meaningful ceremonies and efforts to train new Scouts. [*Herbie Hawk News*, April, 1988]

Recruiting an Active Unit Committee

How active is your Unit Committee?

This is a more important question than you might think. One person can carry a Cub Pack or a Scout Troop by themselves for a little time without the help of others. Sometimes they can do this for a year or so. But the day always comes when that one person burns out. We prove this over and over again every year. Carrying the Scouting program directly to boys as part of the youth ministry of your church or as the youth outreach of your chartering institution is just too big a job for one person to handle.

Every Unit Leader should and must have help. The way for you to provide this help is to have a strong, active Unit Committee. Make sure also that your Unit Committee gets trained.

Remember it is easier to recruit members of the Unit Committee on an ongoing basis than it is to try to get just the right person to be Cubmaster or Scoutmaster in a crisis situation. [*Herbie Hawk News*, May, 1988]

Important Committee Functions

In a recent column I told you about the importance of the Unit Committee to your Unit's success. Now I'd like to discuss two very important committee functions.

The first is to support the Pack or Troop's advancement program. One of our duties toward our young people is to help them build their self-esteem. Scouting's advancement program is designed to do just that. By handling the administrative part of advancement the Unit Committee can support the Unit leaders and provide a vital service to their Unit. An active advancement chairperson on your committee will not only be a big help to the Unit leaders but will be able to actively promote advancement in your Unit.

The second function is to support the outdoor program. Whether this means Day Camp and outings for the Cub Scouts or a year-round camping schedule plus summer camp for the Boy Scouts, this is an integral part of the Scouting program. A strong camping chairperson (or camping subcommittee) can not only be a great help to the Unit leaders by handling the administrative jobs but can also promote the Unit's activities.

If you don't have someone doing these jobs on your Unit's committee, why don't you recruit someone this month? [*Herbie Hawk News*, June, 1988]

First Class — First Year

We promise a great deal when a boy joins Scouting. We promise him fun and adventure. We promise ourselves that we'll help this young boy grow into manhood, equipped with skills and values that will serve him all of his days.

All of our hopes and promises, however, will go for nothing, if we do not try to make sure he stays in the program. Studies have shown that, if a Scout does not reach First Class within his first year in Scouting, the odds are that he won't spend a second year in Scouting.

For this reason, we are placing a special emphasis on First Class attainment. There are a number of aids available to you to help you achieve the goal of helping each Scout reach First Class within his first year. These include the pamphlet, "First Class Emphasis" and the new First Class Certificate.

None of these things are really new but they will help to remind us of the various opportunities that are available to us at every activity to help boys advance. With just a little more effort we can help every boy reach the goal of First Class in his first year and also help him to travel First Class the rest of his life. [*Herbie Hawk News*, September, 1988]

Scouting Skills

Did you ever wonder why the founders of Scouting included so many outdoor skills in the Scouting program? The reason is that these skills are exciting and they are fun to learn. Not only that, but they are essential for being a part of the Outdoor Adventure of Scouting. Through learning of these skills a boy begins to develop the self-reliance that is so important to his growth.

These Scouting skills; knots, identification of plants and animals, cooking, knife and axe, hiking, and pioneering are an integral part of our program both in Cubs and Boy Scouts. Therefore, please make sure that Scouting skills are a big part of the program in your unit. Demonstration of Scouting skills by Boy Scouts make an exciting program at a Pack meeting. Learning and using these skills make an exciting program for your Troop.

Remember, it is excitement and fun that will keep the boys in our programs and it is only when we keep them in the program that we can help them to become citizens of fine character—physically strong, mentally awake, and morally straight. [*Herbie Hawk News*, October, 1988 and again in November, 1988 I must have missed the publication deadline.]

Recruit the Very Best

This month I'd like to talk about recruiting quality Unit leaders for your Cub Pack or for your Scout Troop. Many Units complain that they have a difficult time recruiting new Unit leaders. Part of the problem, I suspect, is that we don't realize just how important a job it is that we're trying to fill.

After all, what is the job of the Unit leader? Isn't the job of a Unit leader to develop quality leaders for the future? Isn't that what Scouting is all about? Isn't it our aim to give our youth the values and skills that they'll need to make tomorrow a better place not only for themselves but also for the community around them?

Therefore, we need the very best person that could possibly be available. Take the time to think about who would be the very highest qualified person for your Unit. Decide who could best approach that person. When you ask, be sure to let your candidate know that you need them because they are the most qualified and that being Unit leader calls for a high quality person.

Remember, quality leaders build quality leaders both for tomorrow and for today. [*Herbie Hawk News*, December, 1988]

Training

Last month we discussed some of the aspects of recruiting a Unit leader. This month I'd like to say a few words about something that your Unit leader should do after taking on the job. No organization in the world could possibly provide more training opportunities than the Boy Scouts. We have Fast Start Training. We have basic Unit leader training and many, many other training courses that are offered. [The training curriculum has been revised several times since this was written. The idea expressed here, however, is still valid.] Each month in every District we offer Roundtables that are an excellent training experience. Think of that; a monthly training course held right in your District.

Yet, as I write this, only 47 of 131 Cubmasters are trained and only 70 of 137 Scoutmasters are trained in the Hawk Mountain Council. Being Cubmaster or Scoutmaster is much too important a job to do without being trained. I urge you to take the training that is available to you. [*Herbie Hawk News*, January, 1989]

Webelos to Boy Scouts Transition

One of the great strengths of Scouting is that it includes activities and programs for boys of all ages; Tiger Cubs for 1st grade boys, Cub Scouts for boys in the 2nd through 5th grades, and Boy Scouts for the older boys.

Each of these programs offers different adventures that appeal to boys at that particular stage in their development. For example, for the Cub Scout aged boys this means a program that includes games, songs, skits, crafts, and other activities with their families. For Boy Scouts this means camping, hiking, running a troop by the Scouting method, and boy leaders deciding what activity THEY think is fun.

What a tragedy it is, then when a boy misses the opportunity to experience it all. What a tragedy it is, when a Cub Scout drops out of the program before he gets to be a Boy Scout.

The way to prevent this tragedy is to make sure that our Webelos make the transition to Boy Scouts. We can accomplish this if the Cub leaders, especially the Webelos Den leaders, take every opportunity to introduce your Webelos to the Boy Scout program. In addition the Troop leaders should also take every opportunity to open the window of Scouting adventure so that Cub Scouts can see what lies ahead of them.

Let's all work together to make sure the transition from Webelos to Boy Scouts happens. [*Herbie Hawk News*, February, 1989]

Scout Uniform

Scouting is a uniformed movement. I mention this for those who haven't noticed. Baden-Powell in *Scouting For Boys* said:

"The Scout kit, through its uniformity, now constitutes a bond of brotherhood among boys across the world."

"The correct wearing of the Uniform and smartness of turnout of the individual Scout makes him a credit to our Movement. It shows his pride in himself and in his Troop."

The Scout uniform reminds the world that the wearer is a Scout and it reminds the boy when he wears it that he is a Scout. This will influence his behavior. He'll act the way he knows a Scout should act.

The Scout uniform is also a great leveler. Scouts come from all different backgrounds, some richer, some poorer, but in uniform they all are a part of the world brotherhood of Scouting.

For many Scouts the cost of the uniform will be a problem. However, if you determine that your unit is going to be in uniform, your boys will, with your help, find a way to get a uniform.

Encourage uniforming in your unit. Start a uniform exchange. Encourage money earning projects to allow your unit to become a uniformed. Hold inspections. All of this will strengthen the Scouting spirit in your unit. Above all, set the example by being in uniform yourself. [*Herbie Hawk News*, March, 1989]

Simple Secrets to Having an Exciting Active Program

Some of you have told me that I'm in a rut. All I ever write about is the importance of a good solid program to the success of our Scouting Units. Well, for those of you that feel this way, this letter is going to give you more evidence that I'm stuck on the same theme.

If you are going to influence a boy; if you are going to help a boy grow to manhood with moral, mental and physical strength, then you are going to have to have him with you on a regular basis. If a boy never comes to your Unit's meeting, then you have no chance to influence him.

The only way that you are going to have a boy with you is if you have an exciting program. It is also no secret as to what constitutes an exciting program. What boys are looking for is an opportunity to do things in the out-of-doors. They will tolerate indoor activities, if they lead to an outdoor activity. Give your boys an opportunity to plan an outdoor activity every month if you have a Troop or plan frequent outings if you have a Pack. These are the simple secrets to having an exciting active program in your unit. [*Herbie Hawk News*, May, 1989]

What is a Commissioner?

I am as excited about Scouting today as I have ever been. As I write this, I have just returned from a three day College of Commissioner Science Conference at the Lancaster-Lebanon Council's Camp Mack. With me at this Conference were twenty of your unit commissioners, assistant district commissioners, and district commissioners. The dedication of these people to Scouting is the vibrant vital force the helps you make Scouting work for the youth of our communities.

Just what is it, you may wonder, that a commissioner has to do that these men and women would be willing to take a whole weekend away from home? What is this service that commissioners perform for units?

The job that your commissioner has to do is to provide personal friendly service to your unit. This is to help you insure that Scouting is available to the maximum number of boys. The duties of a commissioner are:

A. Know the Scouting programs,
B. Visit your unit's meetings,
C. Visit with your unit leader,
D. Visit with your unit committee,
E. Keep in touch with the chartered organization,
F. Know the neighborhood,
G. Know the district and the council,
H. Set the example,
I. Continue to grow in experience and knowledge.

All this is to help you successfully use the Scouting program.

Now all this training has to be used. So give your unit commissioner call, if you have any questions, or if there is something that you'd like to have help with. While you're at it, take the opportunity to tell your commissioner how much you appreciate his or her help. [*Herbie Hawk News*, July/August, 1989]

Thank You!

The thought came to me as I visited summer camp that our Scouts were really having a great time. If you spend only a few minutes in the dining hall at supper time, you hear only animated conversation and laughter. Summer camp is a fun time and our Scouts are enjoying it.

My next thought was that all of these kids will grow to become either Scout leaders or parents of Scouts or both. When that time comes, they will realize just how much work and time and effort that you, their leaders, put into Scouting. They will realize just how many hundreds of hours that you spent working to make their unit a wholesome experience for them. They will realize just how much of your life was spent in meetings and on campouts with them.

When that realization comes, they will want to thank you for all that you've done for them. Until that time comes, on behave of our Scouts, let me say thank you for them. Thank you, from the bottom of my heart, for all that you're doing for Scouts and Scouting. [*Herbie Hawk News*, September, 1989]

Hazing

I WANT TO DELIVER A VERY CLEAR MESSAGE.

Hazing, harassment, or bullying have NO place in Scouting. This says it all but I'm afraid that some will get the wrong idea. I'm not necessarily talking about big guys beating up on smaller guys. You all know that that's not proper and work to prevent it.

What I'm referring to are the little hurts that add up to big hurts that will mean that some young Scout has an unpleasant experience in Scouting. I'm talking about name calling. I'm referring to sending a young tenderfoot Scout out to find a "left handed smoke shifter." I'm talking about things like these that many units have tolerated in the past.

To many of us these things seem minor and just part of the game. The fact is, they're not minor to the small boy who is in our care. We're just going to have to think again about what's going on. These things are not in keeping with the Scout Law—A Scout is Friendly. These supposed minor things mean an unpleasant experience for a young Scout and they mean that he will not stay with us long enough for us to be a positive influence on his life.

Think about what goes on in your unit. Eliminate hazing, harassment and bullying. Instead emphasize the importance of the fellowship of Scouting. Make Scouting a positive experience for ALL of the Scouts, not just the bigger few. [*Herbie Hawk News*, October, 1989]

A Successful Scout Unit

There is no secret to having a successful Scout unit, whether it is a Cub Pack, a Scout Troop, or an Explorer Post. The ingredients are two. The first is a leader who respects young people. Our youth will be quickly turned off by anyone who does not respect them, who talks down to them, or who does not listen to their ideas. The second factor is an exciting program. With these two ingredients, young people will flock to your unit.

Logically, you might ask, "Just what constitutes an exciting program?" The answer to that is easy, too. We have to the put the adventure, that we promised, into the program. As it has been put so many times, "We have to put the 'outing' back in Scouting." What our kids really want to do is, "Play in the dirt and eat bugs." Any unit's program, Pack, Troop, or Post, that doesn't allow them to do just that will not be successful. When dealing with Scouts and Explorers, you must also give them a chance to do their own planning.

So take a look at your unit. Is it everything that you had hoped? If not, the answer may lie in the program. Add more adventure, more outings, more hikes, and more campouts. See if that doesn't help things. [*Herbie Hawk News*, November, 1989]

Youth Ministry Exploring

We have an occasion for joy in our Council that I'd like to call to your attention. We have, in the last few weeks, chartered two new Explorer Posts, the first to St Peter's UCC Church in Wilshire and the second to St John's Lutheran Church in Boyertown. The emphasis of these two posts will be Youth Ministry Exploring. The exciting thing is that this represents a new use of the exploring program in this council and a relatively new use for exploring nationally.

These churches will use the exploring program as their youth fellowship. Some of the advantages to using exploring in this way are: 1) a framework of organization already in place which includes multiple unit leaders and a unit committee; 2) a plan for youth leadership and youth planned activities; 3) access to Scouting camps and other facilities; and 4) leadership training for both youth and adults.

The program of these units will be: Bible and other church related studies; service projects; social events; and outdoor adventures, such as campouts, hikes, and ski trips. All of these will be programs and activities planned by the youth themselves. This is a traditional use of a Scouting program. These explorer posts become an integral part of the youth ministry of the chartering churches and provide them with an opportunity for outreach to the youth of the community. [*Herbie Hawk News*, December, 1989 Today we would call this a Venture Crew]

The '90's

Scout Sunday

I would like to address this message to the churches that charter one of the Scouting programs.

Every year in February we celebrate the founding of Scouting with Scout Week. As a part of Scout Week, we also recognize Scout Sunday. This is a good opportunity to celebrate your use of the Scouting programs as part of your youth ministry and your outreach to the youth of your community.

You can start this celebration by inviting all of your Cub Scouts, Boy Scouts, Explorers, and their leaders to a regular service. At this service you can recognize the leaders, present the unit's charter and/or recognize the accomplishments of some of the youth.

This not only serves as a way to thank the leaders but it also helps remind the congregation that the Scouting programs belong to them and are a part of the church's youth ministry. If a Sunday during Scout Week is not a good time for your church then hold you celebration of Scouting at another time. [*Herbie Hawk News*, January, 1990]

Roundtables

My grandfather used to tell me that the three most important things that contributed to a successful drug store were; 1) location, 2) location, and 3) location. The same sort of thing can be said about a successful Scouting unit, whether it is a Pack, a Troop, or a Post. The three most important things that contributed to a successful Unit are; 1) program, 2) program, and 3) program.

Now where, you might ask, can you get help to make sure that your unit has a good program? The answer, my friends, is very simple. The answer is Roundtables!

Every district is working to develop better and better roundtables. If you're an old-timer, you'll pick up some ideas that will mean a more exciting program in your unit. If you're a new unit leader, you'll be exposed to an unending supply of new ideas. Roundtables are held monthly in each district. Please attend. It's important. [*Herbie Hawk News*, February, 1990]

A Scout is Cheerful

As you surely know, Scouting was started by Lord Baden-Powell. When Baden-Powell was growing up in the mid 19th century, it was very popular for boys to write down their "Rules for Life." One such rule that a young Baden-Powell, "Lord Bathing Towel" to his young companions, wrote in his diary was, "I must try to be cheerful under all circumstances." When he wrote *Scouting for Boys* forty years later this became, "A Scout smiles and whistles under all difficulties." Today this is a part of the Scout Law and we say, "A Scout is Cheerful."

For what Baden-Powell knew was that anyone can be a grouch. It takes no special effort to grumble and complain, whenever anything goes wrong. But if you have a song in your heart, and a smile on your lips, when it's raining, and you're tired, and your feet hurt, then you will be sure to have more fun in life.

Now one of Baden-Powell's favorite stories was *Peter Pan*. If you remember this story, you may recall that Peter Pan was afraid to grow up because he was afraid that adults didn't know how to have fun. But you know that the young people in our Scouting programs do not have to afraid to grow up as Peter Pan was. They will all know the secret to a happier life, because we have taught them Baden-Powell's Rule "...to be cheerful under all circumstances." [*Herbie Hawk News*, March, 1990]

"Recruiting Is Easy!"

Many of you have recently told me that you're having difficulty getting adult volunteers to help with your unit. I'm really surprised at this since it's so easy to recruit scouters. WHAT? You say you don't believe me when I say, "Recruiting is easy!" Well, the fact is that recruiting is easy when you follow the scouting method—"The Six Sure Steps to Success in Recruiting." These steps are:

1. **Call a Meeting of the Knowledgeables**—That is, call a meeting of people who knowledgeable about Scouting and your community.

2. **Hold a Meeting**—Hold a meeting of your Knowledgeables and decide what the requirements are of the job you're trying to fill and what kind of person would be best for the job. Make a list of these criteria.

3. **List and Appraise Prospects**—Make a list of all of the people who would be a good prospect. Then make an assessment of how each prospect

meets the criteria you set up as your guide to the kind of person you were looking for. Make sure the institution head approves these prospects.

4. **Appoint a Subcommittee to Recruit the Leader**—Your appraisal should make it clear who is the best candidate. Decide who is going to do the actual recruiting.

5. **Make an Appointment with the Prospect**—Set up a time for the subcommittee to meet with the prospect.

6. **Call on the Prospect**—Call on the prospect at the appointed time and sell the benefits of the job.

Continue this process until the job is filled. If you try this the next time there is an opening for a leader in your unit, you'll see how easy recruiting is. [*Herbie Hawk News*, April, 1990]

A Bonus in My Scouting "Pay-Check"

Those of you that have been Scout leaders for any length of time know that your Scouting "pay-check" comes in many forms. Mostly, it comes in the form of that look of confidence that appears on the faces of our Cubs, Scouts and Explorers, as they learn to deal with life on more than even terms. Sometimes, though, we do wonder if we really make a difference.

Well, I recently got a bonus in my Scouting "pay-check" that I'd like to tell you about. I got a call from one of my former Scouts. He now lives in Florida. He has a wife and a baby girl. He's an Assistant Scoutmaster for his local Scout troop. He said that he just called to say, "Thank you." He's just now beginning to realize how much work went into being Scoutmaster and he's now beginning to realize how much it meant in his life.

So you see my friends, we do make a difference. Every hour and every day that we spend with our Cubs, Scouts and Explorers make a vast difference in their lives. Keep up the good work, all of you. [*Herbie Hawk News*, May, 1990]

Active Unit Committee

How active is the committee for your unit? How many people attend your regular committee meetings? Having an active committee is one of the keys to a successful Cub Pack, Scout Troop, or Explorer Post. [Today we would say—Venture Crew] For example,

Does your Cubmaster get involved with more than running the Pack meetings, training other leaders, and helping with the Pack program plan?

Does your Scoutmaster have to do anything more that train the boy leaders and advise them as they proceed with the troop program planning?

Does your Post Advisor get stuck doing more than training the Post leaders and helping them plan the Post program?

If you've answered, "Yes," to any of these questions, then you've got your unit leader doing things that should and can be done by an active committee. By not spreading the work out among more people you run the danger of causing "Unit leader burn-out."

Only two courses of action are open to you. Either develop a stronger more active committee or get a copy of "The Six Sure Steps to Getting a New Unit Leader." Sooner or later not getting help will cause a unit leader to retire. Get busy on this, please; our young people are depending on you. [*Herbie Hawk News*, June, 1990]

Building Character

A recent article in the *Philadelphia Inquirer Magazine* profiled the actor, body builder, and businessman, Arnold Schwarzenegger. It discussed his meteoric rise from the hard times of post WWII hardship to his present status as a movie superstar and chairman of the President's Council on Physical Fitness. When asked to characterize the way that he had overcome adversity, Arnold said, "You build character through resistance the same way that you build muscle in the gym. The more resistance it meets the more it will grow."

As I thought about that quote, I realized that this is exactly what we do in Scouts. We put young people in positions and places where their character meets resistance. We put our Scouts in the woods on a Friday night trying to pitch a tent in the dark. We put them in situations where they get chosen for leadership. We let them test themselves at their own pace against the advancement system. And we recognize their successes. All of this "resistance" helps their character grow.

The more active your unit is the more situations arise that provide the "resistance" that builds character.

Therefore, make sure your unit has an exciting, varied program. The future of your Scouts, the future of your community and, indeed, America's future depends on this. [*Herbie Hawk News*, September, 1990]

Scouting is a Game

Baden-Powell, the founder of Scouting, told us that Scouting is a game. Games as you know are meant to be FUN. Thus, the idea is that Scouting has to be fun to be effective. It has to be fun for the boys and it also has to be fun for the adults as well. This is a fundamental idea in Scouting and something that we sometimes forget.

This does not mean, of course, that there are no serious aspects to Scouting. What is does mean is that the fun doesn't stop just because we are dealing with something serious. As we prepare young people for an adult life there is no more lasting legacy that we can give them than to teach them to enjoy all aspects of life and to have fun in whatever they're doing. There are already enough sourpusses in this world. Let's try to make sure that our Scouts and Cubs are not counted among them. Let's make sure that as our Scouts learn the Scout Law that they learn to pay special attention to "A Scout is cheerful." In this way they'll learn to have fun and enjoy life in all that they do.

For yourself, in those moments that you're not having fun, check to see if you've forgotten that Scouting is a game. If you've forgotten to have fun, what will you be teaching our boys? [*Herbie Hawk News*, November, 1990]

Scouting Makes a Difference

I was reminded recently through a chance encounter with one of our local educators that Scouting really does work. He said that in school they always know which were the boys who were in Scouts. The boys didn't have to be wearing their uniform. It was their actions that exposed their Scouting experience. The boys with Scouting experience were the ones who showed leadership. They are the ones who are less likely to get into trouble. They were the ones who had confidence in themselves.

I don't know why I needed to be reminded about this. It's just that as we go about the "business" of arranging meetings and going to summer camp and going on campouts, we sometimes forget the fundamental reason that Scouting exists, the fundamental reason that we're in the Scouting movement; to help young people grow into adulthood equipped to be responsible and useful citizens.

Scouts are the ones that are prepared. Scouts are the Cub Scout that saves his younger brother's life. Scouts are the ones that stop to help someone in trouble. And why do they do these things? They do them because these are the things that we've taught them to do. These are the things that we've showed them by our example.

So my message to you is—Keep up the good work! Scouting does make a difference. Your long hours as a Scout leader make all the difference in the world—to the future of the world. [*Herbie Hawk News*, December, 1990]

Advancement Recognition

BEWARE! BEWARE! THIS IS A WARNING! The rumor mongers have been at work again. Someone has been telling some of you that Cub Scout and Boy Scout advancement awards can only be recognized once and that the best time to do this is at an annual Court of Honor or at an annual "Blue and Gold" dinner. Please be warned;

THIS IS NOT TRUE. WE NEED YOUR HELP IN GETTING THE WORD OUT TO EVERYONE.

The purpose of the advancement program is to provide our youth with recognition for their accomplishments. There are too many times in their young lives that we are at great pains to tell them what is wrong. The advancement system gives us a chance to tell them about things that are right ABOUT THEMSELVES. There are too many instances in their daily lives that they are in competition with others. The advancement program gives them a chance to measure themselves against a standard at their own pace. To be REALLY effective recognition must come quickly. The promise of recognition later is not enough and misses a great opportunity. Recognition should also be made often. Announce his accomplishments at the very first opportunity; even if you can't give him a badge. You can announce his accomplishments again and give him the badge at the next meeting. Announce his awards at the next Court of Honor or at the annual "Blue and Gold." Make the annual event a time to give summary recognition for all of the year's awards. Put an announcement in the unit's newsletter. Put an announcement in the Church's newsletter. Send a news release to the local paper. Read the advancement report at a church service. Can you think of another way to multiply the recognition you can give a boy for one award? When one of our boys accomplishes something, make a big, big fuss. Each and every one of them really deserves it.

Now that you know about these rumors, I hope that you will help me to squelch them. Tell everyone that you talk to about advancement that the purpose is recognition. Remember that you can't give too much recognition. [*Herbie Hawk News*, January, 1991]

Boys' Life

This is the time of year that we are involved in that wonderful activity called "Rechartering." As you and your unit work on the rechartering process for your unit, I'd like you to give special consideration to *Boys' Life* magazine. *Boys' Life* is a special part of the Scouting program and of the Scouting method. Among the reasons that *Boys' Life* is so special are:

1. *Boys' Life* helps our boys with reading. As parents and as Scout leaders we all know how important reading is to the development of our Scouts.

2. Illiteracy is one of Scouting's unacceptables. A personal subscription to *Boys' Life* is a valuable incentive for a boy to develop a reading habit.

3. Receiving *Boys' Life* magazine helps a new Cub or a new Scout feel that he is part of the unit.

4. *Boys' Life* is the largest circulation youth magazine in the world. Every issue is jam-packed with articles of interest to our boys. Boys look forward to receiving getting their copy in the mail. Don't take my word for this; ask a few of your boys.

5. A subscription to *Boys' Life* is a valuable tool that helps maintain a boy's interest in Scouting. It can be a part of the adventure that we promised him.

6. *Boy's Life* can help insure that a Cub Scout continues into Boy Scouting

If your unit was not a 100% *Boys' Life* unit last year, please try to make it one this year. If your unit was 100% last year, keep up the good work. Let's work together to make Hawk Mountain Council 100% *Boys' Life*. [*Herbie Hawk News*, February, 1991]

The Value of Scouting

When you are recruiting new adult leadership, you need to tell them the value of our programs. We know this value and that's why we're involved, but sometime we have a difficult time articulating it. Perhaps you need to ask a Cub Scout or Boy Scout that you know, what they think the value of Scouting is. Listen to what one 14 year old had to say. Below are portions of a statement about the value of Scouting, written several years ago by 14 year old First Class Scout Fred Gregory.

"Scouting...is a fascinating adventure that makes men of us by helping us to be boys.... We learn to work together...to respect each other and to be unselfish...to be independent...to help other people and to discover that helping brings more pleasure than anything.

"We find out what America is really like, and we love it.... We grow strong in body and clear in mind.... And we have such a good time doing it all.

"That is why I say, that, next to a boy's family and church and maybe his school, Scouting is the best thing that a boy can get into."

Our friend Joe Davis, Philmont Scout Ranch, Director of Camping (1965-1975) recently submitted the above to *Scouting Magazine*. Eagle Scout Fred Gregory is now a NASA astronaut. [*Herbie Hawk* News, March, 1991]

The Reason Scouting Exists

The reason for Scouting to exist is that it gives us a chance to influence a boy's life. We get a chance to set the course that he will follow. In many ways the Scouting program itself takes care of this without any special effort on our part. We need only follow the program. The patrol method, the advancement program, the Scout Oath, and the Scout Law all combine as the background setting to help develop a boy's character, fitness and citizenship. This is the magic that Baden-Powell has given us to work with.

All of this is the smooth flowing stream of Scouting opportunities to help mold a boy in the way that we would have him go. Sometimes, however, our Scouting stream must flow over some rocks. These rocks also provide opportunities to mold a boy. In the course of our meetings and outings, our boys will sometimes do the things that boys sometimes do. Dare we mention it? Some will on occasion lie, cheat, steal, destroy property, act in a rowdy manner, and otherwise treat each other in an unfriendly way. Do not disparage these times. Use them. Don't deny that something has happened. These are the golden moments when your actions and reactions can shape a boy's life. Your firm, kind counsel can make the difference. Make the best of these opportunities to show a boy the right road to travel. And above all don't ignore the situation. To do that is to waste an opportunity, a golden moment, given to you to set a boy on the path to a successful life. Your strength as a Scout leader to act in these situations is what sets you apart from other men and women. [*Herbie Hawk News*, September, 1991]

Advancement

Advancement is the backbone of the Scouting programs. Through advancement a boy receives recognition for his accomplishments. These accomplishments should come as a natural outgrowth of the other activities in the unit. Thus, if a unit has an exciting program and opportunities are present for advancement, then boys will advance. Because they advance they will receive deserved recognition. This will increase their self-esteem and help them grow into responsible adulthood.

Thus the boy through the exciting program receives the adventure that we promised him. At the same time we have achieved our aims and given him the tools he will need as an adult. It is such a simple formula and it works just as Baden-Powell said that it would. And of course most of you know all of this very well.

If we follow the prescription of exciting activities and the opportunity for advancement, we'll see the majority of our boys reaching the maximum level of recognition, the Eagle rank, at 14 to 15 years old and not at the 17 to 18 years old level we now see. And we should see more reach this level of recognition potential, if we can find ways to help the boys make the activities more meaningful.

More excitement and more opportunities for advancement; these are the ingredients that will make Scouting more viable in our community. Let's make a maximum effort to achieve this. It's only the future of the world that we're working toward. [*Herbie Hawk* News, November, 1991]

Synthetic Scouting

> Personally I fear there is a danger that a kind of
> synthetic Scouting may creep into our training in place
> of the natural article described in *Scouting for Boys*. I
> would urge District Commissioners to watch out for
> this in the course of their inspections and correct the
> tendency where they spot it.
>
> By "synthetic scouting" I mean the Scout system
> obscured by overclothing the natural form with rules
> and instructive literature, tending to make what
> originally was, and should be, an open-air game into
> a science for the Scouter and a school curriculum for
> the boys.

The above may sound as if it was written just yesterday
but, in fact, it was written in 1936 by Lord Baden-Powell,
the founder of Scouting. Scouting is a game. Anything that
we do that makes Scouting for our boys less of an outdoor
game and more like a school room scene, the less likely we
are to be successful. Furthermore, it is easy to measure our
success. Boys vote on our programs with their feet. If our
programs follow the prescription that B-P gave us, they will
stay with us. If we do not, we'll find that the boys will find
other things to do. Scouting is not about "teaching" boys
things. Scouting is about boys having adventures. While
they are having these adventures, we are able to inculcate
in them values of character and citizenship that we agree
are important.

Take a close look at the program in your pack or troop.
Make sure that the scouting in your unit is the real stuff and

not "synthetic Scouting." [*Herbie Hawk* News, December, 1991]

Make Scouting Resound "With Jolly Laughter"

In 1932 Lord Baden-Powell, the founder of Scouting, wrote:

> I'm not satisfied, although one might think I ought to be.
> Our numbers are steadily growing—training centres increasing; Scout spirit good; and so on. But there is too much leakage, and also too little character-growth—as yet. Leakage of Cubs not going up to Scouts; Scouts not going up to Rovers, etc.—this come from many causes. In some cases it is difficult to remedy, but in many cases the reason is that boys have become tired of Scouting. With an understanding Group Scoutmaster this seldom happens. But where the same old programme, or want of programme, goes on week after week, and month after month, boredom is only natural.
> Where the Scouter is himself a bit of a boy, and can see it all from a boy's point of view, he can, if he is imaginative, invent new activities, with frequent variations to meet the boys' thirst for novelty. Note the theatres in London. If they find that a play does not appeal to the public, they don't go on hammering away with it in the hope that it will in the end do so; they take it off and put on some new attraction.
> Boys can see adventure in a dirty old duck-puddle, and if the Scoutmaster is a boy-man he can see it to. It does not require great expense or apparatus to devise new ideas; the boys themselves can often help with suggestions.

Where a troop resounds with jolly laughter, and enjoys success in competitions, and the fresh excitements of new adventures, there won't be any loss of members through boredom. Then outdoor camping—not merely occasional sips of it, but frequent practice so that the boys become experienced campaigners—will hold those of the best type and will give a healthy tone to their thoughts and talks.

I have little use for a cut-and-dried routine in a Scout Headquarters building, with its temptations to softer living and parlour Scouting.

What B-P wrote in 1932, quaint spelling and phraseology aside, is just as true today as it was then. Make your unit, pack or troop or post [crew], resound "with jolly laughter" and enjoy "the fresh excitement of new adventures" and you will surely be a great success and the boys we recruited in September will still be with us next September and the September many years from now. [*Herbie Hawk News*, January, 1992]

The Scouting Programs Are To Be USED

I'd like to address this message to the parents of our Scouts. Our good friend in Scouting Glenn Piper publishes a newsletter, *Scouting Around*, for Pack and Troop 529 in Gibraltar. A couple of months ago his lead article reminded me of a very important aspect of the Scouting movement. This is that the Scouting programs are to be *USED*.

We often encourage churches to *USE* the Scouting programs as a part of their youth ministry and as their outreach to the youth of the community. We forget to ask parents to USE the Scouting programs as one of their tools for raising their kids. As Glenn tells the story, he had a parent come to him and ask which Troop events were most important for their son to attend. At first he thought he'd have to say which was more important than another. Then it occurred to him that here was a busy parent taking time to ask about the Scouting so that they could most effectively *USE* the Scouting program to benefit their son.

So to the parents I say, "You want your son to develop high moral values, to know the importance of physical and mental fitness, to have strength of character, to develop self-esteem and to develop confidence in himself. *USE* the Scouting programs as one of your tools to accomplish this. Work with your Scouting leaders to make the program even better so that you can make even better *USE* of Scouting."

The Scouting programs are meant to be *USED*. *USE* them to make your son better prepared for the future. Work with your Scouting leaders to make your Scouting an even better tool. [*Herbie Hawk News*, April, 1992]

Reading

Let's talk about *READING*. We all know that one of the unacceptables is illiteracy. Yet every year we produce 2.3 million new illiterates. The results are that 85% of the juvenile offenders are illiterate; 50% of the unemployed are illiterate; and 50% of the prison inmates are illiterate.

Getting your boys to read *Boys' Life* can help make sure your boys don't contribute to these statistics. Why *Boys' Life*? Because it stimulates awareness of the Scouting Program and extends the Scouting experience. It has an impact on the whole family and reaches four additional readers for each subscriber. *Boys' Life* delivers the challenge of high adventure and promotes reading which is so important to a boy's future.

In a recent survey of *Boys' Life* readers 74% had advanced a rank in the past year compared to a 68% national average. Sixty-nine percent went to summer camp compared to 36% of all Scouts. And the average tenure of *Boys' Life* readers was 4.3 years compared to the national average of 1.7 years. Thus we see that *Boys' Life* readers experience even more and better Scouting.

Help kids win in life by letting them read *Boys' Life*.

Your unit has just rechartered. If you didn't recharter as a 100% *Boys' Life* unit, now is the time to get *Boys' Life* subscriptions for all of your boys. Make your unit 100% *Boys' Life*. [*Herbie Hawk News*, May, 1992]

Scoutmasters, Make Listening Your Occupation

"A further way of discovering activities that will appeal to the boys is for the Scoutmaster to save his brains by using his ears." This is as true today as it was when Baden-Powell gave us this advice in 1922. It is easy to find out what boys want to do. They signed on for the Scouting adventure and they know what that's all about. Listen to their ideas about what an exciting Scouting program should be. If you let them plan the activities, if you let them take responsibility for what your unit does, then you will be a success. This is the Scouting method and it works.

Baden-Powell went on to say, "...if you make listening and observation your particular occupation, you will gain much more information from your boys than you can put into them by your own talk.

"Also when visiting parents, don't go with the idea of impressing on them the value of Scouting so much as to glean from them what are their ideas of training their boys and what they expect of Scouting or where they find it deficient.

"The joke about new Scout activities is that they are just like the new toy that daddy brings home for the kiddies; daddy is the first to take to playing with the toy himself. Well, that is just the way it should be in Scouting." [*Herbie Hawk News*, July/August, 1992]

Missed Opportunities

I'd like to talk with you today about missed opportunities. We have our aims and goals in all that we do and yet, we often miss opportunities to achieve those aims. The aim of Scouting is to build the character of our young people. The method of doing this advocated by our founder, Lord Baden-Powell, was to have this development of character come from within the boy rather than from without. We do this by putting the boys into situations where we can observe them and interact with them as they challenge the world. This is the reason that we take our boys to summer camp. As we observe our boys in action we see them do things that we are very proud of. These are the moments that we must treasure and for which we must offer praise.

But what about the other opportunities; the times when they do things that we are not so proud of. Sometimes we miss these opportunities. When our boys do something that we'd rather they didn't do, we let our natural disappointment get in the way of this opportunity to help our Scouts grow. We fail to react. We make excuses. We fail to set limits. We fail to counsel. We let an opportunity to help a boy grow, to set a boy back on the road to adulthood slip away. The saying, "Boys will be boys," can either be an excuse to ignore misdeeds and do nothing or it can be the opportunity to forge another link in the chain of character built on the principles of the Scout Oath and Law.

When boys do the things that boys will do, use that time to gently put them back on the right path. After all, this is why we took them into the woods in the first place. To have fun was their reason. Our reason is to build character. [*Herbie Hawk News*, September, 1992]

A Scout Is Welcome

The poet Robert Frost once wrote:

"Home is the place where,
When you have to go there
They have to take you in."

Scouting should be like that home of Robert Frost's. Whenever a boy goes to one of our units, we will make him welcome, no matter what. He will find people who are kind to him there; it's our law. He will find people there who are friendly; it's our law. He will find people who are helpful there; it's our law. He will find people who are courteous to him there. He will find people there who cheerfully accept him; it's our law.

Whenever a boy goes to one of our units, we will make him welcome, no matter what; it's our law. He knows that no one will pick on him because he is different or smaller or for any reason; it's our law. There is no initiation or rite of passage to be a fellow member in Scouting. A boy has only to say, "Here am I, let me join," and we will make him welcome.

Showing by personal example that we obey the Scout law is what makes Scouting different and what can make a difference in a boy's life. This means that no boy gets picked on, or teased. No boy gets degraded or humiliated. No boy gets sent for "shore line" or for a "smoke shifter." No matter what happens to a boy at school or how he is treated at play, or at home, for that matter, when he comes to Scouting, we make him feel at home. Is this what happens in your unit? If not, perhaps what you have is not truly Scouting but some other kind of boy's club that neither Baden-Powell nor I would recognize. Please think about this as you bring Scouting to our boys. [*Herbie Hawk News*, October, 1992]

Court of Honor

I had lunch with my good friend George Hasker the other day and he gave me what I think is a really swell idea. Perhaps you'll like it too. The next time you have a Court of Honor, why don't you make it for both the Cub Pack and the Scout Troop?

It seems to me that this idea has something for everybody. The most important idea behind advancement is that the boy gets recognition. Recognition for doing the very best he was able to do. With the combined Pack and Troop presentation there will be more people involved, hence more recognition. Remember we can't make too much fuss about a boy's advancement. Fuss is the main ingredient.

Next, we are always struggling to get more of the boys that are in Cub Scouting into Boy Scouting. Sometimes the boys seem to think that after a few years in cubs that they've seen it all. Perhaps an occasional glimpse of Scouting at a Court of Honor will be just the ticket to whet their appetites for a full course meal of Scouting later on.

Finally, getting the Pack and the Troop and all of their families together seems like the makings of a pretty good party. And any excuse for a party is a good one. Try this out for your next Court of Honor. Let me know how it works out. [*Herbie Hawk News*, November, 1992]

Boy Leadership

I have a vision of what real Scouting looks like. Apparently many of you have this same vision too because I see real Scouting when I visit your unit. Scouting is a place where they accept you for what you are. Scouting is a place where you can build your confidence and self-esteem through the things that you do. Scouting is the place where boys run things and the job of the adults is to train boys to do this. This is a unique aspect of Scouting. There is no other program in the world that offers our young people this opportunity.

During a recent visit to one of our units, I observed that throughout the evening the adults present were in the back of the room. They participated only when they were called upon by the boys who were running the program. Such leadership skills do not happen by accident. You have to train your boys to accomplish this. It is harder work in the beginning than doing it yourself. As time goes on, however, boys who have seen the example of older boys leading the troop learn from these older boys. The most important lesson that they learn is that it is possible to be a leader. Furthermore, trained boy leaders will train the next generation of boy leaders. When this happens, you will have the Scouting that Baden-Powell intended that you should have.

If your unit is not boy run, work to make it so. The greatest adventure of them all is learning to be a leader. This is the Scouting adventure. Make it possible for your boys. [*Herbie Hawk News*, December, 1992]

"Let them eat cake"

Maria Antoinette said, "Let them eat cake." I say, "Let them fail." "What," you say, "let them fail! Why, that's so messy and it will scar them for life." "Stuff and nonsense," I reply. When I was a Scoutmaster, (long ago and far away) I would often get phone calls from the mothers of new Scouts. "What should Johnny take with him on the campout?" Answer, "Whatever he wants." "But what if he should forget something?" "Well then, he won't forget next time." The point, if I may belabor it for a moment, is that, if we let Johnny fail in this controlled situation where he can't get hurt by his failure, then he may just learn something. The very least he may learn is not to make the same mistake again. Hopefully, he may learn to plan through all of his actions such that he'll never "forget something" that he needs, ever.

Remember that these are the methods of Scouting. Don't be too quick to jump in and make things run smoothly. If things run smoothly, then there is no opportunity for learning. If things are a little rough, then there are plentiful opportunities for learning. "Let them fail," I say. "Let them eat cake," too. That sounds like fun! [*Herbie Hawk News*, April, 1993]

Letter to My Grandsons

This is a letter to my grandsons about why I think they should join Boy Scouts. Since none of them will be needing this for a few years yet, perhaps you might find a use for it in the meanwhile. [*Herbie Hawk News*, May, 1993]

Dear Grandson,

There are a number of really good reasons why I think you should become a Boy Scout. Some of these are reasons that will be understandable to you now. Others are ones that you may not appreciate now but, when you're older, they will seem more important to you.

First of all are the reasons that you'll understand now. You should become a Boy Scout because it's a game and you'll have fun. This is the most important reason of all. If you don't have to, why spend your time doing anything that isn't fun? Scouting is an adventure that involves camping, hiking, swimming and many other fun things to do. You will also have an opportunity to be recognized for what you can do, not for what others may expect of you. As you advance through the ranks of Scouting, you may even someday become an Eagle Scout.

You may not understand this now but when you're older you'll appreciate that Scouting allowed you to associate with boys like yourself, who were learning to develop physically, mentally and with strength of good character. This association with boys like yourself will not only help you grow but will keep you from influences that might otherwise lead you astray. You will also learn to love your country and your God. You will learn to seek out opportunities to be of service to your fellow man. Best of all, none of these things, will detract from the fun of Scouting now!

I hope this will help each of you decide to become a Boy Scout. Remember, whatever you decide, I love you.

Your Grandfather,

Planning

What is the difference between a unit that is really great compared to one that is not so great? The answer of course is PROGRAM. I've written to you many times about this in the past. This time I'd like to discuss one of the secrets of having a great program. Please pay close attention to this because it is a secret that most of you know, but sometimes forget.

The secret that I want to reveal to you now is PLANNING. I know that what you're saying now is, "Come on! I know that planning is the secret to having a successful program. What's so special about that?" Well, what I'd like to suggest to you is that you take a few minutes one night at camp this summer with your Patrol Leaders Council and plan the outline of the year's events. As a minimum, plan a theme for the month and plan your monthly outing or campout. By doing this at camp your boys are caught up in the spirit of Scouting and will do a better job. After the troop leaders have done this they can share the results with the rest of the Troop and get immediate feedback from the rest of the boys. In this way the boys plan the activities when they're in the best frame of mind and the plan gets wide dissemination within the unit. With this basic plan outline for the year in hand the monthly planning sessions will be much easier. Let me know how this works in your Troop. [*Herbie Hawk News*, July/August, 1993]

The Lesson for Today Is Advancement

School is now in session. The lesson for today is advancement. Advancement is a major part of the Scouting program. It was there from the beginning, not added on later. Baden-Powell had advancement at Brownsea Island. The purpose of the advancement program is to find a way to recognize our Scouts; to acknowledge their achievements. Advancement is not a test. Advancement is recognition. Now, please go to the black board and write this down 100 times!

Advancement is not a test. Advancement is recognition.

Advancement is not a test. Advancement is recognition.

...

Advancement is not a test. Advancement is recognition.

Recognition to be most effective must be timely. If a boy earns a badge tonight, tell everyone TONIGHT. Let him wear it! This gives him recognition. When you hold the quarterly Court of Honor with all of the parents present, recognize him again. Advancement is recognition. When you hold the annual Court of Honor and troop or pack banquet, make a fuss over him again. Let the parents applaud for every boy individually. Advancement is recognition.

Give awards for advancement in a quick and timely fashion. Give recognition often. You can't give recognition too often. Let me say that again. It is not possible to give recognition too often. Advancement is recognition.

If a boy earns a badge at camp, hold a Court of Honor at camp and give him the badge at camp. Whatever obstacles you believe exist that prevent having a Court of Honor at camp, find some way to overcome them. When a boy earns tenderfoot, hold an impressive ceremony. When a boy earns First Class, make a big deal about it.

If a boy earns the Eagle rank, hold at least two ceremonies. One in church and one at a separate court of honor that is just for him alone.

Check the blackboard where you wrote—

Advancement is not a test. Advancement is recognition.

Advancement is not a test. Advancement is recognition.

...

Advancement is not a test. Advancement is recognition [*Herbie Hawk News*, September, 1993]

Those Golden Moments In Scouting

Our good friend in Scouting, Earl P. Moyer, pointed something out to a group of us the other day. I thought I might share it with you. There are those golden moments in Scouting, when a boy comes to you, at a meeting or on a campout, when he feels a need to have your undivided attention. These are the moments when he wants to show you his accomplishments or share his thoughts with you. It is times like these that are the focus of Scouting. Our aim is to influence a boy's character for the better. When these golden moments come, you must be ready. You cannot be too busy. You cannot be preoccupied with something else. You must take that moment and give it to a boy who needs you. You must praise his accomplishments. You must respect and acknowledge his thoughts. You must not waste that golden moment.

This is one of the methods of Scouting. You are there with that boy as a role model. You are there to influence his character. You are there to show him the way. It is your presence that he is responding to. It is your presence that he is responding to when he expresses a need share his thoughts or his accomplishments. At that golden moment he trusts you to respond in a positive way to his need. At that moment you cannot turn him away. Be trustworthy. Be loyal. Be kind. Be friendly. Be prepared. Waste not that golden moment. [*Herbie Hawk News*, October, 1993]

Were you there?

There was a clean dampness in the air because it had rained heavily in the predawn hours. As the dawn broke, the rain stopped and a lace-like mist hung over the lake. In the early light the fall foliage, reflected in the calm waters, looked as if it were painted under a slowly bluing sky. A pair of geese were making a noisy announcement that they were taking off for their dawn patrol.

Were you there? Did you see this? Were you witness to this majestic display of nature's splendor? Does this scene sound familiar to you? Have you taken your boys to see this? Is camping and hiking a major part of your troop's program? If so, great! If not, you need to work on your program. Learning to appreciate the outdoors is part of the adventure that we promise those who join scouting. It is in the outdoors that we can get the opportunity to work on the character development of our young people. Therefore we need to be sure we keep the outing in scouting. [*Herbie Hawk News*, November, 1993]

The Peace Movement

The season of the birth of the Prince of Peace is upon us. As is the custom for this time of year, I'd like to give you my Christmas greeting. Our founder, Lord Baden-Powell, once wrote, "The only really practical step so far taken... [toward world peace] is in the Boy Scout Movement, where, with our brotherhood already established in every country and getting daily into closer touch and fellow-feeling by means of correspondence and interchange of visits, we are helping to build the foundation for the eventual establishment of common interests and friendships which will ultimately and automatically bring about disarmament and a permanent peace." In other words, if all the world is linked through the ideals of Scouting, we can no longer have armed conflict. If every boy is brought to adulthood believing in the Scout oath and the Scout law, who will break the peace. Perhaps you never thought of Scouting as a peace organization, but when the boys of every nation reach out to one another with the Scouting handshake of friendship, who will go to war.

So, I thank you for the work you have done in the past year toward world peace through Scouting. I thank you for the work you'll do in the year ahead as we bring quality Scouting to more and more young people in the Hawk Mountain Council. [*Herbie Hawk News*, December, 1993]

The Patrol Method

The heart and soul of the Scouting Movement is the Patrol and the Patrol Leader. There are still some of you who do not understand how much a boy can do. And you'll never find out because you never give him a chance. It's instructive, I think, to look for a moment at what our founder, Lord Baden-Powell, had to say on this subject in April, 1910.

> Some few Scoutmasters are still behind the time, and consequently their Troops are behind the average, in not making sufficient use of their Patrol Leaders.
> They ought to give the sub-officers [boy leaders] as much liberty of action as they like to get themselves...
> They must hold the Patrol Leader responsible for everything good or bad that occurs in his Patrol.
> They must put responsibility upon him, let him do his job, and if he makes mistakes let him do so, and show him afterwards where he went wrong—in this way only can he learn.
> Half the value of our training is to be got by putting responsibility on young shoulders. It is especially valuable for taming the wilder spirits; it gives them a something which they like to take up instead of their equally heroic but less desirable hooligan pursuits.

So don't let your Troop get "behind the average." Give your boys the "heroic" task of taking responsibility. Above all, let them make mistakes. This is the hardest thing of all to do. It will help, if you remember that we're not in the business of running smooth meetings and disaster free campouts. Our objective is to mold the character of our young people. If it will help a boy leader's development, let things run amuck for awhile. Make the boys take responsibility. In this way the boys will have "the value of our training." [*Herbie Hawk News*, January, 1994]

"Last night!"

I saw this story recently in a newsletter that I get called *Leader Lore*. I thought I might share this story with you. It is a story Gene Bowden told of walking downtown during a break between some meetings, still in his Scout uniform.

"Hey mister! Are you a Scoutmaster?" a lad asked him excitedly.

"Well, sort of..." Gene said (he was National Director of Boy Scout Programs).

"Well, I'm a Scout." the boy continued. "We go camping and on hikes in the back country. We stalk deer and build high lookout towers and go canoeing and we've got the neatest patrol flag! You ought to see our patrol flag! Helped make it myself!!"

"My, that's wonderful, son, when did you join?"

The boy paused, looking him in the eye, his head shook kind of firmly from side to side as he said with determined youthful vision, "Last night!"

"Last night!" Can you imagine it? Can you imagine a young boy saying that? True Scouting can only take place when the vision that a boy had of the adventure that we promised becomes a reality. True Scouting can only take place when a boy gets the fun and excitement that he thought he was going to get when he joined. All that Scout leaders have to do to make that vision a reality is to train boy leaders and stay out of their way. Trained boy leaders will plan exciting programs because they are boys themselves. They know what excites them. When all of this happens, boys will stay in Scouting. Then we will have the time to try to influence their character. Then we will have the time to train them to be good citizens. This is Scouting's method. [*Herbie Hawk News*, February, 1994. I had an almost identical experience in 2006. I met a new, just-joined Cub Scout at his cousin's Eagle presentation. His enthusiasm is a treasure that must be invested to grow at compound interest, not frittered away.]

Don't SEND Your Sons to Scouting

This is an open letter to parents who are thinking about letting their sons join either Cub Scouts or Boy Scouts. My advice to you is; don't *SEND* your sons to Scouting. You may think that Cub Scouting is about crafts and songs. You may have heard Cub Scouting is about the Pinewood Derby and about having fun. That sounds like fun, doesn't it? Still, my advice to you is; don't *SEND* your sons to Scouting.

You may think that Boy Scouting is about letting your son go camping and learning the craft of the wood. You may have heard that Boy Scouting is about summer camp and hiking. That sounds like fun, doesn't it? Well, my advice to you is; don't *SEND* your sons to Scouting. And, of course, you may have heard that many boys in Boy Scouting really enjoy it and that some even advance to become Eagle Scouts. These certainly sound like wholesome, worthwhile activities, don't they? This may be true but my advice to you is still; don't *SEND* you sons to Scouting.

You have surely heard that Cub Scouting and Boy Scouting are all of these things. And as far as a boy is concerned, they are! BUT THAT'S NOT WHAT SCOUTING IS ABOUT. Scouting is the training ground for the character of your sons. Scouting is about a boy gaining confidence in himself. Scouting is about learning a value system. Scouting is about being prepared for life. If this is what you want for your sons, please don't *SEND* your sons to Scouting. COME WITH THEM! Help us in our task. Help us build the character of your sons. Remember, "Character counts!" [*Herbie Hawk News*, March, 1994]

Are You Using The Right Kind Of Bait?

If you're going to catch something, you need to bait the trap with the right kind of bait. When I was a boy growing up in Maryland, we used to go down to the Chesapeake Bay and fish for crabs. The Maryland blue crab is delectable. Those of you who have not partaken of this delicacy have really missed out. The equipment that you need for crabbing is a piece of string, a crab net and a couple of chicken necks. You tie the chicken necks on the string and dangle them in the water. Crabs love the chicken necks. They grab on to them. As you slowly pull the string in, they continue to hold on. When they come within reach, you can get them with the net. Chicken necks are the right bait for crabs.

The promise of adventure draws boys to Scouting. When they have joined, the fulfillment of that promise is what keeps them there. They love an active outdoor program. Boys love to go camping. They love the confidence that they feel when they are progressing through the ranks of the advancement program. I've never yet seen a boy frown at a Court of Honor. They love the pride that they feel when they take positions of leadership. They love being in a gang; in the fellowship of Scouting. Outdoor adventure, self-confidence, fellowship, and a feeling of pride in leadership are the right bait for boys. Are you using the right kind of bait in your unit? Show me the size of your catch. Maybe that will tell us something. [*Herbie Hawk News*, May, 1994]

Return To The Summit of Scouting

A recent week long business trip to Mexico gave me two days of sitting in airports, which was a good time to catch up on some of my reading. One of the books I got to finish was *Return To The Summit of Scouting; A Scouter's Midlife Journey Back to Philmont* by William Cass. Bill Case was an Eagle Scout in Troop 40 in the old Lancaster County Council. During summers in his college years he was on staff at Philmont. He is now active in Scouting in the Chester County Council. Bill recently returned to Philmont as an advisor for a crew that included his Eagle Scout son. He had been told by our friend "Hab" Butler that of the many summits of Scouting "going through Philmont with your son is the highest." As Bill tells the story, he may just be right. *Return To The Summit of Scouting* is the story of these sojourns at Philmont. He not only tells a lot about the magic of Philmont but also manages to tell us of the spirit of Scouting that has been the guiding light of his life and of his family. Bill's story is not only a memoir of his high adventure but also an example of life lived to the fullest.

If you have ever been to Philmont, or if you might ever go someday, this book is a must for you. If someone in your unit is planning a trip to Philmont, this book is a must for you. This is must reading. [*Herbie Hawk News*, June, 1994]

Recruiting Additional Adult Volunteers

This month I'd like to talk about recruiting additional adult volunteers into Scouting in your unit. Many of you have told me that your biggest problem is getting enough help in your unit. In many cases you have a unit leader and you have a committee chairman. What you need are more committee members and more assistant unit leaders. You also have told me that when you approach people to help out, you get turned down. Yet you know, or suspect, that the people that turn you down, do have the time and would enjoy helping with Scouting, just as you do.

Perhaps the problem is that we're not being subtle enough when we make our pitch. When you ask someone to be a committee member or an assistant leader, perhaps they don't know enough about the position to make a favorable decision. A more subtle approach would be, for example, to ask a prospective candidate for an assistant leader position to come to a meeting and help with a specific project. Or you might ask them to come along on a unit outing. Or you might ask a committee prospect to help with a few phone calls. If everything works out, you then ask them to do something else. And if that goes according to plan, you again ask for help in some small way. If this goes on long enough, they won't be able to say they don't have time. Nor will they be able to say they just don't know enough about how to do the job. This is because they'll already be doing the job. Now if you can get all the other committee members working on a few other people in this way, you'll soon have a full committee. If you can get the other assistant leaders trying to recruit a few others for your unit, you'll soon a large number of assistant leaders. Remember that many hands make labors light! Try to be more subtle about this in the future. Good Luck! [*Herbie Hawk News*, September, 1994]

Have a Jolly Time

It is now approaching that time of year when we all wish each other a joyous holiday season and that is my wish for you. It is my sincerest wish that all of you have a jolly holiday and that you have a jolly time in Scouting in the year ahead.

"Jolly" is a word that isn't used that much anymore. To me it connotes happiness and having a cheerful fun time. It is a word that appears often in the writings of our founder, Robert Baden-Powell. Thus it is a most appropriate word to use when talking about Scouting. Isn't having fun and having a jolly time what Scouting is all about? If Scouting is fun, young people will stay involved. Then we will have an opportunity to influence their character. Then we will have an opportunity to show them the road to good citizenship. If Scouting is fun, then adults will stay involved longer. Doesn't "A Scout is cheerful," imply that we should have fun in everything we're trying to do?

Thus it is essential that all aspects of Scouting be fun. Building character, a serious subject, is the aim of Scouting. Having a fun, jolly time is our method and it is what attracts both youth and adults to the Scouting programs. So make sure your Scouting programs are fun. Have a jolly time and enjoy the holiday season! Have a fun time and enjoy Scouting throughout the year! Have fun in everything that you do. It's the Scout Law! [*Herbie Hawk News*, December, 1994]

Advancement

Long ago and far away, when I was a Scoutmaster, the mother of one of my newest Scouts called me and asked, "What should my little boy take on the campout?" I told her then, as I would tell her today, "He should take what he wants." If he forgets something, he'll remember it the next time. [If you're around me long enough you'll hear me repeat all of my stories. I've used this one in at least two other essays.] We teach boys what to take on a campout. It is the first requirement for Tenderfoot, to know what you want to take on a campout. Thus the advancement system is about teaching boys things and about them learning things. Right? Well, no, that's wrong. Advancement is about boys achieving self-confidence.

To be a Second Class Scout, a Scout must show how a compass works. Does this mean that the advancement program is about learning how to use a compass? No, it doesn't. Even though years later one of the things that a man will remember is that as a Scout he learned how to use a compass, this is not what it's about. It is fun to learn how to do things and a boy doesn't even notice that he got confidence in his ability to do something on his own in the process. It is that measure of self-esteem that defines the advancement program. This is the magic of Scouting. This is what it's all about.

We teach boys to how to pack their backpacks for campouts and trips into the woods. What we really hope we've accomplished is that we have helped them pack their minds and their hearts for the journey into life. This is what is the purpose of advancement.

For advancement to be fully effective in its purpose, the boy needs to get recognition. Would you work for no pay? Would you work if you didn't get a pay check? Well, think of the recognition as the pay check for advancement and let me ask the same question again. Would you get excited about advancement if you didn't get any recognition? The point is that you must recognize a boy promptly for his achievements. And you must recognize him often. If you recognize a boy for achieving confidence and self-esteem, you will be fulfilling the purpose of the advancement program. [*Herbie Hawk News*, January, 1995]

Living by the Boy Scout Oath and Law

I was recently in Gibraltar to make presentation at an Eagle Court of Honor. One of the other presenters was our State Representative, Mr. Sam Rohrer. Mr. Rohrer told a story about the time when he was deciding to run for state office. One of the things that he did was that he personally called about 150 registered voters. One of the questions that he asked was, "What kind of person do you want as a representative in Harrisburg?" Some of the answers that he got were, "Someone who is honest (trustworthy)," or "Someone who is helpful." Others answered, "Someone who won't waste our tax dollars (thrifty)." Still others answered, "Someone who lives by the Boy Scout ideals." In all 75% of the voters that Mr. Rohrer contacted indicated, either directly or indirectly, that they wanted someone who lived by the Boy Scout Oath and Law.

This is a wonderful story and I'm delighted that Mr. Rohrer could share it with us. It indicates that the public knows about the work that you are doing. They know of the efforts that you are putting forth to try to shape the character of the youth of our community. They believe that you will be successful. And more than that they agree with our goals and ideals. Keep up the good work, all of you. The young people of our community are depending upon you. [*Herbie Hawk News*, March, 1995]

Two Tiny Wooden Beads on a Leather Thong

About Wood Badge Green Bar Bill [William Harcourt] wrote:

Two tiny beads on a leather thong doesn't sound like an outstanding badge and mark of distinction. But it is known and respected as such around the globe. It is symbolic of the efforts and interest of one man on behalf of others that created and launched the greatest movement for boys the world has ever known.

It is the mark of those who demonstrated that they are men and women of character and who are devoted to a cause. Men and women who strive for perfection well knowing that even the best is not enough. Men and women who hold the welfare of others before self. Scouters who live up to all that name implies. Awarded to a Scouter on the basis of what he or she thinks and is, more than on knowledge. They must demonstrate that they have "Know How," too! Good intentions count for little until by application of ability and determination they produce results that count. Striving for perfection in themselves that they might train others better. To this end exists Wood Badge.

It is doubtful that the thought ever entered the mind of Robert Baden-Powell that his efforts on Brownsea Island would grow to influence the youth of the world and that in the days ahead thousands of men and women would carry his efforts toward an ever increasing number of boys.

Who knows but that this effort, this crusade, may flourish to the end that two tiny wooden beads on a leather thong may yet become the symbol of a succeeding effort to bring about a World Brotherhood under God. To that end may Wood Badge serve and her men and women never falter or fail. Two tiny wooden beads on a leather thong. They could symbolize the hope of the world. It's up to you.

Are you Wood Badge trained? No! Please sign up now. It's up to you! [*Herbie Hawk News*, April, 1995]

A Letter to Alice

Dear Alice:

You asked me the other night at the Wood Badge Feast what my inspiration was for these monthly letters. The answer is that my inspiration is people like you and Ron who are keeping the Scouting promise for so many of the young people in our community.

When a young man joins Scouting, we make him a promise. We make a promise of adventure. We make a promise of fun. We make a promise of wholesome activities. The way that you and Ron, and hundreds like you, keep that promise for the young people that you come in contact with is an inspiration to me.

When a young man joins one of our programs, we make a promise to his parents. We promise them that the Scouting program that he joins will be a quality program. We promise that that program will be a help in the development of his character. You and Ron devote a significant portion of your lives to keeping this promise. You and the hundreds of others that do the same are a great inspiration to me.

When a young man joins Scouting, we make a promise to our Chartered Partner that we will help them with their youth ministry and/or with their outreach to the youth of the community. You and hundreds of other are doing that every day. You, Alice, are my inspiration. You, Ron, are my inspiration. You have kept the promise to our Scouts. You have kept our promise to the Scout's parents. You have kept our promise to our Chartered Partners. It is easy to write these letters with inspiration like that. [*Herbie Hawk News*, May, 1995. Not only are Ron and Alice Bortz long time Scouters of great renown, wonderful parents and delighted grandparents but their seats at the Reading Royals Ice Hockey games are quite near mine.]

Patrol Leaders

"Some few Scoutmasters are still behind the time, and consequently their Troops are behind the average, in not making sufficient use of their Patrol Leaders.

"They ought to give the [Troop Boy Leaders] as much liberty of action as they like to get themselves..."

"They must hold the Patrol Leader responsible for everything good or bad that occurs in his patrol."

"They must put responsibility upon him, let him do his job, and if he makes mistakes let him do so, and show him afterwards where he went wrong in this way only can he learn."

"Half the value of our training is to be got by putting responsibility on young shoulders. It is especially valuable for taming wild spirits; it gives them a something which they like to take up instead of their equally heroic but less desirable hooligan pursuits."

Lord Baden-Powell had a way with words and a way of explaining the value of the Patrol method. The paragraphs above are as true today as they were in April, 1910 when he wrote them. Take a look at the activities in your Troop. If Baden-Powell came to visit your Troop, would he think you were "making sufficient use of [your] Patrol Leaders." [*Herbie Hawk News*, June, 1995]

A Boy's Behavior

A boy's behavior is our opportunity. What he does and how you react to what he does is what will shape his character. Baden-Powell said:

"The whole object of our Scouting is to seize the boy's character in its red-hot enthusiasm, and weld it into the right shape and to encourage and develop its individuality— so that the boy may educate himself to become a good man and a valuable citizen for his country."

"Don't let the technical outweigh the moral. Field efficiency, backwoodsmanship, camping, hiking, good turns, jamboree comradeship are all means, not the end. The end is *character*—character with a purpose. And that purpose, that the next generation be sane in an insane world, and develop the higher realization of Service, the active service of Love and Duty to God and neighbor."

The words of our founder are as much to the point today as they were over fifty years ago. Try, as difficult as it will be, to keep all of this in mind when things get really intense at camp this summer. Take the opportunity to let a boy's behavior give you the opportunity to mold his character. Remember that character is our aim—not a smooth running campout. [*Herbie Hawk News*, July/August, 1995]

Letter To My Grandson

This is a letter to my grandson about why I think he should join Cub Scouts. Since I don't think my oldest grandson is going to need that much persuading and my other grandsons won't be needing this for a few years yet, perhaps you might find a use for it in the meanwhile. [*Herbie Hawk News*, September, 1995]

Dear Grandson,

There are a number of reasons why I think you should become a Cub Scout. Some of these reasons are ones that you will understand. Others are ones that you won't understand now but you will when you're older. First of all you should join because Cub Scouting is fun. I know from first hand experience that Cub Scouting is fun because I was a Cub Scout when I was your age. You will be with a lot of your friends in Scouting and together you and your friends will have lots of adventures. One of the things I know you'll enjoy is going to Scout Camp in the summer. There you'll get to swim, shoot arrows and BB guns. You'll get to earn badges and pins to put on your uniform.

All of the above are things that you'll understand now. When you get older, you'll appreciate that in Scouting you'll develop your character. You'll learn to be self-confident and self-reliant. You'll learn to be a good citizen. And you'll develop personal fitness; mentally, physically and morally. As I said, these are not things that are important to you now but you will understand when I say that these are things that will make your parents very proud of you.

I hope that you enjoy Scouting as much as your Father did.

Your friend,

Grandpop

Anonymous Letters

Recently a friend of mine in Scouting received an anonymous letter. Since some really nasty things were said about him in this letter, he was naturally upset. I told him that he should follow the rules that I follow when I get such at letter.

Rule 1: Read the letter only for amusement.
Rule 2: Don't take anything in the letter seriously.
Rule 3: Take no action based on an unsigned letter.
Rule 4: Discard after reading.

I also assured him that the letter could not have come from a Scout or Scouter. By way of proof of this I referred to the Scout law.

A Scout is Helpful. Such a letter is not intended to be helpful.

A Scout is Friendly. To say nasty things about someone is not friendly.

A Scout is Courteous. Nor is it courteous.

A Scout is Kind. Nor is it kind.

A Scout is Brave. Not signing your name to a letter is not particularly brave.

I hope you'll agree that I gave my friend good advise and that you'll think about this any time you should get an anonymous letter. [*Herbie Hawk News*, November, 1995]

My Christmas Gift to You

The Christmas season will soon be upon us. It is the custom to give gifts at this time of year and many of you are, no doubt, wondering what I'm going to give you this year. You must wonder no longer. You'll not have to wait. Right here and now I'm going to tell you about this year's present. My gift comes in three parts. The first part is **knowledge. Knowledge** is a gift that once received; it can only be used or not used. It can't be broken or thrown away. **Knowledge** of the ways of Scouting comes in many forms.

We have training for almost every aspect of Scouting. We have so much training that "We'll get you training," is almost a cliché in our movement. This year I'd like you to have training in the Scouting programs, Cub Scouts and Boy Scouts. These training programs will be held in your District once a month for the next year. We call these sessions **Roundtables**.

The second part of my gift to you is **fellowship**. I've arranged for the unit leaders of our Cup Packs and Scout Troops to get together once a month in each District to enjoy each others company, to share their successes with each other, and learn from each other. This **fellowship** of Scouting we call **Roundtables**.

The third part of my gift to you is the **Spirit of Scouting**. You can catch the **Spirit of Scouting** at any Scout meeting but it will especially be available to you at the monthly **Roundtable** in your District. The exact time and location is announced elsewhere in these pages. It is especially appropriate for you to receive the **Spirit of Scouting** in this season of the Prince of Peace for Lord Baden-Powell, the founder of Scouting, believed that if all the world would catch the Spirit of Scouting and live by the Scout Oath and Law that there would be peace in the world.

Remember, for you to make full use of my this year's gift to you this year you must attend your District's Roundtables regularly. I'll see you there. [*Herbie Hawk News,* December, 1995]

"Uniform Police"

I don't care what anyone tells you—there is no such organization in Scouting as the "Uniform Police." It is one thing for a Scout Troop to decide that for the sake of uniformity, they are going to all wear a certain cap. It is all very well for them to decide on a particular neckerchief. Troops should decide which of the uniform options they are going to adopt. This is an important use of the method we use in Scouting called—the Uniform.

There are some people who, however, have read the Uniform Guide. They believe that it is a revelation from on high. They develop a myopia that has them convinced that their copy was carved in stone before the beginning of recorded time. They will delight in telling you that such and such a patch must be worn 3 millimeters to the left of where you happen to be wearing it. Get a life! Our aim in Scouting is to develop character, citizenship and personal fitness. We should not waste our energy on anything that doesn't help us toward that goal. And there is no logic which postulates that moving that patch one millimeter will further the cause.

So, the next time you run into someone who thinks they're a member of the "Uniform Police," demand identification. When they can't produce it, make helpful suggestions about things they should do to get on with their life and be a help to the Scouting movement. [*Herbie Hawk News,* January, 1996]

Your Unit Commissioner

I'd like to talk to you today about your Unit Commissioner. Early in the Scouting movement, Baden-Powell found that many unit leaders were having difficulty learning what their jobs were and how the Scouting movement was supposed to work in influencing the character of the boys who joined. To help him make the Scouting movement grow he appointed a County Commissioner for each county.

These were the first commissioners in Scouting. Their job then was the same as is the job of a commissioner today; to help a unit prosper. In order to accomplish this the Unit Commissioner visits the units to which he or she is assigned. They try to keep the unit in touch with what's happening in the District and in the Council. They try to keep their eye out for problems and provide the help that a unit needs to weather any storm that might arise. In short they try to be a resourceful friend to their Packs, Troops and Posts.

In order to be prepared to do this important job the Unit Commissioner usually has considerable experience in Scouting. They take special training and attend special conferences to help them prepare to help you in your Packs, Troops and Posts.

Thus we see that your Unit Commissioner is important to the health and growth of your unit. They are there to help you provide a strong program for boys in your Pack or Troop, or for the young people in your Post. In this way your Unit Commissioner is your ally to help you so that you will be able to influence the character and personal growth of these young people. Why don't you say a hearty thanks to your Unit Commissioner the next time you see her or him? If you're not sure who your Unit Commissioner is, give your District Commissioner a call. [*Herbie Hawk News,* February, 1996]

Boys' Life

This is the month that we are doing something I know all of you look forward to all year. That's right we're rechartering this month. Isn't that exciting! Isn't that fun! Wow! While we're about it though, there is something that

I'd like you to do. Is your unit 100% *Boys' Life?* I certainly hope so. 100% **Boys' Life** means that every household in your unit receives a copy of **Boys' Life**.

There are a number of reasons for wanting to have all of your boys be subscribers to **Boys' Life**. First of all, boys that take **Boys' Life** stay in Scouting two years longer than boys who don't. That's two years longer to influence their character that you wouldn't otherwise have. *Boys' Life* subscribers advance in rank faster and more often than boys who don't. The boys who get **Boys' Life** are more active in their unit, district, and council events than boys who don't. Boys like reading **Boys' Life**. As Jere B. Ratcliffe, our Chief Scout Executive, has pointed out, "Each month, **Boys' Life** brings to our Scouts a wonderful and exciting world of reading, with articles that help them to become better Scouts. Because **Boys' Life** goes into the Scout's home it brings greater parental and sibling understanding and support of Scouting activities. Get the family involved in Scouting—through **Boys' Life**. Make **Boys' Life** a part of your unit's Scouting program. Make your unit 100% **Boys' Life**. [*Herbie Hawk News,* March, 1996]

Key 7 Review

What in the world is a Key 7 Review? Let's talk first about what it is not first. The Key 7 Review is not an inspection of your unit. It is not the village inquisition. What it is, is an opportunity for you and the other leaders in your unit to discuss your plans for the future with the district leadership. It is an opportunity for you to influence the kind of service that you'll get from the district. The Key 7 Review is a meeting between the key unit leadership and the key district leadership. From the unit the key unit leadership is the Unit leader, *i.e*, the Cubmaster, the Scoutmaster or the Advisor, along with the Chairman, and the Chartered Organization Representative. The head of the Chartering institution might also attend. For the district the attendees are the Unit Commissioner, the District Chairman, the District Commissioner and the District Executive.

At this meeting I expect that you'll discuss the history of your unit and your plans for its future. You should expect that you'll also discuss how the district can help you achieve your goals for the future.

Thus the Key 7 Review is an opportunity for the unit leadership and the district leadership to influence the future of the unit. It is an opportunity for both the unit and the district to make sure that everything is being done to bring Scouting to the youth of your community. Make the most of this opportunity. [*Herbie Hawk News,* May, 1996]

A Boy's Behavior

A boy's behavior is our golden opportunity. Our aim in Scouting is to improve, as much as we can, a boy's character. And that is why the summer months in Scouting are so important. During these months we get to spend a great deal of time with our Scouts; more time than usual; more time than during the rest of the year. We get to observe how our boys react to the various situations that we place them in. All of these activities are the cauldron in which we mix the life experiences that shape a boy's character.

However, we can't be just passive onlookers and observers of what a boy is doing and how he's doing it. We need to react. We need to interact with him. That's why his behavior is our opportunity. It's our moment to let him know that we've seen what he's done. If he's done the things we want him to do, then we need to let him know about this. A boy will advance farther with praise for what he's done right than he ever will being damned for what he's done wrong. As my Grandmother used to say, "More flies are won with honey than with vinegar." So when you see behavior that you approve of, be sure to let the boy know, specifically, what you saw and liked.

If he's done something wrong, that's the time for the friendly, helpful coach in you to come out. When boys have come out on the wrong end of a situation, that's the time they need and want a friend. At the same time they can do without your anger. What is needed is your help. A boy's behavior is an opportunity, that moment of gold that the whole Scouting experience is set-up to give you. Make the best of these opportunities. [*Herbie Hawk News,* July/August, 1996]

"I Ain't Never Had Too Much Fun."

Daryl Singletary in his new hit Country/Western song "Too Much Fun" sings, "I don't care what anybody says I've done, I ain't never had too much fun." I was reminded of this song the other day when I was talking to my grandson about his experience at Cub Scout day camp. Have you ever been to day camp with your Cub Scouts? I was able to go up to camp this year with my grandson and his Wolf den for two whole days. What a blast! All day we went from one fun activity to another. Unless you've done that you can't imagine how much fun that was for seven year old boys and their seven years old, in spirit, grandfather. Wow!!

This is the kind of thing that binds boys to Scouting.

When they go do something where they have fun all day, for five days in a row, then that kind of activity is the kind that keeps boys in Scouting. And it is during these activities that we get to interface with the boys and we get to influence their character. But they're having so much fun they don't even notice what we're doing. This is the secret to Scouting!

What reminded me of Daryl Singletary's song was that my grandson said when I asked him how he liked day camp, "Grandpop, I think I had too much fun!" So maybe, just maybe, you CAN have too much fun. Why don't you plan right now to make sure your Cubs get to day camp next year? While you're at it, why don't you make plans to go yourself? Adults are allowed to have fun. Maybe, if you're lucky, you'll have too much fun. [*Herbie Hawk News,* September, 1996]

Camps of Proved Desire and Known Delight

Measure the fun that your unit is having. That is the measure of your success. Why is that? The reason is very simple. No boy ever stepped forward and asked for his character to be developed. Yet that is exactly our aim. We want to develop his character. How do we accomplish this? How do we attract young people to our programs and keep them interested? We do this by making Scouting fun. As long as the program is fun, Scouts will stay involved. The longer they stay involved, the longer we have to try to influence them in a positive way. This is the secret of Scouting. Rudyard Kipling wrote ["The Feet of the Young Men" by Rudyard Kipling. The second stanza of this poem used to appear on the Wood Badge Certificate.]:

Now the four-way lodge is opened,
Now the hunting winds are loose
Now the smokes of spring go up to clear the brain;
Now the young men's hearts are troubled
For the whisper of the trues,
Now the red gods make their medicine again

Who hath smelt wood-smoke at twilight?
Who hath heard the birch-log burning?
Who is quick to read the noises of the night?
Let him follow with the others,
For the young men's feet are turning
To the camps of proved desire and known delight!

Make sure that your programs visit "the camps of proved desire and known delight!" In this way you're sure to be a success. [*Herbie Hawk News,* November, 1996]

Look Forward With Hope

In 1937 Baden-Powell, at 81, wrote..."It has been said that youth is fortified by hope and old age is soothed by content. Youth looks forward with hope, old age looks round with content, and some day, when I grow old, I am going to look round with great content. In the meantime you who are not over eighty-one must go on with the work you are doing; there couldn't be better work, and you will be earning your old-age pension of content when you will be able to look back with satisfaction on having done a work that is worthwhile. And to the younger ones I say press forward with Hope; mix it with optimism and temper it with the sense of humour which enables you to face difficulties with a sense of proportion. Press forward with a Faith in the soundness of the Movement and its future possibilities, and press forward with Love which is the most powerful agent of all. That spirit of love is, after all, the spirit of God working within you. Remember, 'Now abideth Faith and Hope, and Love—these three. But the greatest of these is Love.' Carry on in that spirit and you cannot fail."

The work that you do in Scouting is shaping the future of the youth of America and the youth of America will shape the future of the world. May God bless you at this holiday season as He has blessed you to be a blessing to the world? [*Herbie Hawk News,* December, 1996]

How Are The Boys Voting In Your Unit?

Boys vote with their feet to tell you how they like the Scouting program in your unit. I tell you if those feet are "hiking" then those boys will be voting to stay your unit. By "hiking" I mean any activity or adventure that the boys consider to be fun. Usually, though, if there is an outing involved then the boys will consider it to be fun. In a Scout Troop it's easy to determine what the Scouts consider fun. Since they're planning the activities (They ARE planning the activities, aren't they?), it stands to reason that they'll plan something that they think will be fun. Wow, what a concept! In a Cub Pack you have to think like a 9 year old. This should not be difficult for any of our adult male leaders, as any female leader will gladly tell you. You might also ask the boys.

You get the idea. If Scouting is fun, boys will stay in. They'll vote with their feet and stay in your unit. If they stay, in then you'll have an opportunity to influence their character. If Scouting is not the adventure that we promised, then boys will not stay in. They'll vote with their feet to leave the unit. I think that you agree logically, that if their not in Scouting, we have no chance to help develop their character. We'll have no chance to help them grow, mentally, physically, and morally straight.

So I ask you, how are the boys voting in your unit? Are their feet walking in or are they walking out? If "out" is your answer, fix the problem with a more exciting program. Take your boys "hiking." [*Herbie Hawk News,* March, 1997]

Camping

"What should my little boy take on the campout?" This is a question that many Scout leaders have heard from the mothers and fathers of their Boy Scouts. The answer is, "Whatever **he** thinks is appropriate." If **he** doesn't take the right stuff this time, we can be sure that, if **he** had the responsibility for packing his gear this time, **he'll** get it right the next time. The reason that we take Boy Scouts camping is not so that they can have a good time (although they almost always do) but so that they can learn about themselves and about what they are capable of. This kind of experience is age appropriate for 11, 12 and 13 year old boys. Boy Scout leaders are trained to handle this kind of situation. The structure and organization of a Boy Scout Troop lends itself to having a large number of boys in a camping situation. Camping is a venue where we can influence a boy and the development of his character.

Camping, except at Scout camp, is not age appropriate for Cub Scout aged boys. Boys age 6, 7, and 8 are not ready to take responsibility for themselves in the out of doors. Cub Scout leaders are not trained to handle a large number of boys in a camping situation. The organization of the Cub Pack does not lend itself to controlling boys while camping. Webelos Scouts, however, can go on an overnight campout, if the ratio of adults to boys is one to one. That is, one adult for each boy.

It is important that we keep this distinction between Boy Scouts and Cub Scouts in mind if we are going to provide a quality program for our young people. This is why tour permits will not be given for Cub Scouts to camp overnight nor would Scouting's insurance be in force for a Cub Scout overnight campout.

Please call me, if you feel a need to discuss the National Scouting policy on Cub Scout camping. [*Herbie Hawk News,* June, 1997. The official policy on Cub Scout camping has changed since I wrote this a decade ago.]

A Boy's Behavior Is Our Golden Opportunity

The time for summer camp is upon us. As the weather gets warmer, we'll do more and more camping and hiking. The more time we spend out of doors with our Scouts, the more time we have to observe their behavior. And there is one thing that we need to keep in mind. A boy's behavior is our golden opportunity. Scouting is an educational adventure. We've chosen camping as our venue because this draws boys to Scouting like a magnet. Because of the fun and adventure of camping, boys come willingly into our classroom. And what do we teach? We teach citizenship. We teach strength of character. We teach self-confidence. We teach leadership. Our teaching method is to put boys into situations where they can learn by their own experiences and, if possible, by their own mistakes. Your job as a Scout leader is to be the tutor in this classroom. You must observe a boy's behavior. If the behavior that you see is what you like, you need to reinforce it so that the boy will repeat it in the future. If the behavior that you observe is not behavior that you would like to see repeated then you need to let the boy know that also.

In either case it is important that you react to the boy's behavior with kindness and friendship. The boys are looking to you to help them develop. It will not help if you become overly emotionally involve in the process. If you let anger get in the way of helping a boy to understand what he must do to develop his character, you will have missed an opportunity to help a boy grow. Be patient. In time your efforts will be rewarded and the boy will grow in the direction you have pointed. Cherish the moments and the opportunities that are given to you. Use each to the best of your ability. [*Herbie Hawk News,* July/August, 1997]

Baden-Powell Was a Genius

As I watched the Scouts arrive at the Jamboree and set up their thousands of tents, it occurred to me that Lord Baden-Powell of Gilwell, the founder of the worldwide Scouting movement, was a genius. And the fruits of his genius are our inheritance today. The thing that allows us to operate a Scout troop is the inherent organizational structure. A Scoutmaster has a number of assistants to help train the boy leaders. The trained boy leaders then run the troop, handling the bulk of the work, coached and mentored by the adults. This is the structure that Baden-Powell used at the first Scout camp on Brownsea Island in the summer of 1907. One of the exhibits at the Jamboree was a re-enactment of that first Scout camp on Brownsea Island. It was awe inspiring to see how little had changed in 90 years in the basic structure of Scouting. It was very exciting to see boy leadership in action just as B-P used it so long ago. B-P also used the same organization for the Boy's Patrol at Mafeking. This idea of boy leadership is our inheritance from Baden-Powell. It was his genius.

Be sure to use your inheritance wisely and don't squander it by not using it. Let the boys run the troop and use the leadership skills that you've taught them. Being able to lead their own affairs is one of the things that attract boys to Scouting. It also one of the activities that help to build their self-confidence; something that we're trying to accomplish in Scouting. [*Herbie Hawk News,* September, 1997]

Fun, Adventure, Advancement, and a Safe Haven

In Scouting we believe that a boy should believe in God, should believe in his country, and should believe in himself. We try to develop activities that will help a boy grow and that will help him become confident in his own ability. Unfortunately, if you tell boys that you've got a program that will help them develop a belief in God, country, and self, boys will stay away in droves.

However, we don't have to try to come up with a plan for how to attract and keep boys. Lord Baden-Powell, the founder of Scouting, worked that out long ago. His plan had four elements. These are: fun, adventure, advancement, and a safe haven. Fun and adventure are the two shinning stars that initially attract boys. They are part of the glue that keeps boys sticking to Scouting. Advancement is also an element that holds a boy in Scouting. Working toward fixed goals, a boy receives recognition and positive reinforcement when he achieves these goals. This is a powerful force in keeping a boy involved in Scouting activities. Last, but by no means least, in Scouting a boy is among friends who will never mistreat him and who will always treat him with courtesy and kindness. Having such a safe haven is an invaluable magnet whose pulls holds a boy in Scouting.

Having a boy attracted to Scouting and having him remain in Scouting gives us a chance to influence his character. It gives us a chance to help him develop his belief in God. It gives us an opportunity to help him develop a belief in his country. And it gives him an opportunity to develop confidence in himself and his ability to deal with the world. Thus, for your Scouting unit to be successful, you must make sure that fun and adventure are the substance of you unit's activities. You must make sure that your unit has a strong advancement program with every boy advancing every year. It is especially important that first year Boy Scouts reach First Class in their first year. Finally, you must be sure that you unit is a safe haven. There must be no teasing nor hazing. Every adult he meets must be friendly and kind. Nor can this be a sometimes thing. It must be all the time—every time. Fun, adventure, advancement, and a safe haven are the tools that you can use. A hundred years from now the world will be a better place if you use these to give a boy the gift of a belief in God, country and himself. [*Herbie Hawk News,* January/February, 1998]

Scouting Is Not A Place for Competitive Events

Scouting is not the place for winning and losing. Scouting is not a place for competitive events. Remember that in Scouting we are trying to build self confidence. This is one our aims. When we set up situations where someone wins, then we have a situation where everyone else loses. In Scouting our programs are designed so that all of our

Scouts can be winners. In advancement, for example, boys compete with themselves against a standard. All who surpass the standard advance in rank. Thus all are winners. Thus all receive positive reinforcement. Let me give a ridiculous counter-example to illustrate my point. Suppose we said that each troop could only have one Eagle Scout award per year. Thus the first boy to reach Eagle would get the award; all the others would have to wait until next year. Would boys participate willingly in such a program? Some would but most would likely not.

Some of you would argue that it is important to have competition because it teaches about life. And it is true that competition is very much a part of our lives. But our aim is not to teach a boy about life. Our aim is to prepare a boy for a *better* life by helping build his character, by helping develop a belief in God, by helping him develop a belief in his country and, above all, by helping him develop a belief in himself. If in losing, his interest in Scouting flags, he will not be around for us to influence anything. If in losing, he loses self confidence, we will have failed in one of our aims. Let others teach him about competition. There are many who would take up the task. Let us take as our task to teach him to be a winner. Let us be called to strengthen the inner man that is to be by building inner confidence in the boy now. This is the Scouting program. This is the Scouting way! [*Herbie Hawk News,* March/April, 1998]

Uniform Police

I have really exciting news for you. Many times in the past I've told you that there is no such thing as UNIFORM POLICE is Scouting. This will all soon change. Beginning this fall a new program will be started. This program is the

National Uniform Commissioners (NUC) program. NUC's as they will be called will be required to study the new 357 page *Boy Scouts of America Uniform and Insignia Guide* which will be issued is just a few weeks. After paying a special fee they will be given an opportunity to take a written test. The test will include questions on all aspects of the uniform and the proper place to wear certain insignia and patches.

Successful candidates will be awarded special patches which only NUC's will be allowed to wear. The duty of NUC's will be to attend local and national events and observe that Scouts and Scouters are wearing the proper uniform. It will be their duty to confront anyone they see who is not properly attired. If you are interested in this program, you should contact the service center today. Don't delay! [*Herbie Hawk News,* April 1, 1998. This issue circulated in the office but was never published.]

Recruiting Adult Leaders

I was at camp for part of the Order of the Arrow weekend recently. I was enjoying the company of many of you and I got to thinking about what we have to do to recruit adult leaders. We never seem to have enough people involved even though we have over 4,000 adult volunteers in the Hawk Mountain Council. Part of the process in recruiting someone to be a new leader in our movement is to sell them on the benefits of devoting their time to Boy Scouts. All of us have excellent reasons. We must have, and really good ones or you wouldn't be reading this now. However, when we're talking to somebody that we're trying to recruit we often stumble and can't think of good reasons for someone to join us.

One reason that I think is often overlooked is the

comradeship that we experience with other leaders. Of the hundreds of leaders that I come in contact with, most are truly wonderful people. We all share a common belief that we can help a boy as he grows into manhood. We share a common bond in the belief in the Scout Law and the Scout Oath. The fellowship of Scouting Spirit is truly a treasure. The wonder is that we forget to tell people about this treasure when we're asking them to join us. Think of that the next time you're on a recruiting mission. It just might make the difference. *[Herbie Hawk News,* July/August, 1998]

The Lesson Is To Enjoy Life

It may surprise you to learn that I visited a couple of Scout camps this summer. Imagine me doing that! The first camp had been closed for some time when I visited. The camp director had had the idea that if boys could be engaged in activities that were fun and exciting that he could hold their interest long enough to teach them something. He thought that he could help develop their character. He thought that he could teach them to keep themselves physically strong, mentally awake, and morally straight. He thought that he could help them develop a belief in God, a belief in their country and a belief in themselves. If only— if only the program that he used at this camp was exciting enough. Of course, we NOW know that he was right. This camp's director had been none other than Lord Baden-Powell of Gilwell, the founder of Scouting, and the camp I visited was Brownsea Island in England where Baden-Powell held the first Scout Camp for 20 boys in August 1-9, 1907. The ideas that he developed are just as valid today as they were over 90 years ago. If the program is exciting enough and is enough fun, we can hold a boy's interest long enough to have the <u>opportunity</u> to mold his character.

The second camp I visited was our own Cub Scout Day Camp. On the day I took my grandson to day camp it rained all day. (Yes, I know. That's hard to believe, too.) Some of the boys were having fun. Some of them were not. The boys who seemed to be having fun were with adults who did not complain about the rain. The boys that were upset by the weather were with adults who were not having fun simply because it was raining. So here we have the <u>opportunity</u> to teach boys something. Some adults chose to teach boys that you can have fun no matter what the physical circumstances. Others chose to teach boys that happiness is something that comes from circumstances beyond your control. Thus, if you're positive, your Scouts will be positive. If you're negative, your Scouts will always see the dark side of things. Baden-Powell was right. Scouting gives us an <u>opportunity</u>. We can use that <u>opportunity</u> to teach boys the most valuable lesson they could possibly learn. That lesson is to enjoy life. That lesson is that we can enjoy life if we choose to. This is the lesson in "A Scout is cheerful." Or we can teach Scouts that even some trivial outside factors like a little rain can adversely affect our happiness and that we have no control over it. The choice is yours. You can use the <u>opportunity</u> that Baden-Powell has given us anyway that you will. My hope is that you will give our boys a gift of the wisdom to enjoy life to its fullest. [*Herbie Hawk News,* November/December, 1998]

Men and Women Working Together

I met a Scouting family this summer. It was on the ferry boat we took to Brownsea Island when we were in England. The family consisted of mother, father, a little girl about 11 and a boy 9. The mother is Akela (the same as our

Cubmaster) in the 1st Drayton Scout Group. The father is a member of the group committee. The little girl is very proud of being in her first year in the Scouts and the boy is in the Cubs. The wonderful thing to me was that here I was an ocean away from home and I'm meeting people who were working on the same thing that hundreds of families here in the Hawk Mountain Council are working on. They are working to inculcated in their young people the values that they think are most important; values that are important for our youth to carry them into adulthood.

The world over men and women, mothers and fathers, grandmothers and grandfathers are working together to give our young people a gift. That gift is a love of God, love of country, and love of self. We give this gift so that they can become happy, useful and productive citizens of their community, their country and the world. We give this gift to enable them to live up to the duty that they owe to God, country and self.

In this country we have not yet reached the point were our little girls can join our Scout Troops. We have, however, reached the point where men and women are working together in Scouting; working together to achieve a common goal. I mention this because I recently talked with some people who apparently believe otherwise. They believe that we have some gender specific positions in Scouting. It is not so. It has not been so for some time. Those who believe otherwise need to be taking a peek at their calendars. It is not 1948. It is not 1968. Nor is it 1988. Time marches on. It is 1998. The new millennium is upon us and we need to be sure that the youth of the Hawk Mountain Council, and of the world, are prepared. What is important is that we train our young people to uphold the values of good citizenship that we hold dear. What is important is that women and men work together on this important task.

I hope that your holidays were joyous and that you have a prosperous New Year. Yours in Scouting, [*Herbie Hawk News,* January/February, 1999]

Do you hear the echo?

Do you hear the echo? When you go to your Troop or Pack meeting, do you hear an echo of that first Scout Camp at Brownsea Island? Do you hear the sounds of young boys having fun? Baden-Powell's idea was that if we provided a program that was fun the boys, they would want to be involved and we would have a chance to influence their character. Baden-Powell once said:

> "I like to think of a man trying to get boys to come under good influence as a fisherman trying to catch fish. If he baits his hook with the kinds of food he likes himself; it is probable that he will not catch many. He therefore uses as bait food that the fish likes. So with boys: if you try to preach to them what you consider elevating matter, you won't catch them. The only way is to hold out something that really attracts and interests them."

So if you're doing it right, you'll hear the echo that I heard a few months ago as I stood on the spot on Brownsea Island in England where Baden-Powell held the first Scout camp. Down through the years, if you listen very carefully you can hear that sound of laughter and fun. Listen at your next Pack or Troop meeting. Do you hear that sound? Do you hear that echo?

If your meetings are built on fun and adventure, an outdoor program, and *Boys' Life*, then you'll do OK. If your program is fun for the boys, then it will attract boys and they'll want to stay around. Then you'll be able to influence their character. You'll hear the echo of that first Scout camp from long ago. [*Herbie Hawk News,* March/April, 1999]

In the Epping Forest

In the Epping Forest some 35 miles from center city London is a Scout Camp. The camp was given to the British Scout Association and to Baden-Powell by a Scottish District Commissioner, W. F. deBois MacLaren, as a training center. The name of this camp is Gilwell Park. On the morning of September 8, 1919, a 61 year old retired general of the British Army, Robert S.S. Baden-Powell, the founder of the worldwide Scouting movement, stepped into a clearing at Gilwell Park. He raised to his lips the horn of the greater kudu, one of the largest of the African antelopes. He blew a long, sharp blast just as he had done at Brownsea Island. Thus was assembled the first Scoutmasters' training course. At the conclusion of this training B-P wanted to recognize the leaders who had taken the training. To do this he cut apart a necklace of wooden beads that he had found in Dinizulu's deserted hut during the Zulu War in 1888. He presented each of the Scouters with one of these beads on a leather thong.

Today we know this training course for Scoutmasters and other Scout leaders as Wood Badge. Since that first course in 1919 thousands from all around the world have answered the call of the kudu. It is the recognized bond of fellowship among Scouters everywhere. It is a demonstration of Scouting at its best. At the Jamboree in 1997 I met a Wood Badger from Ghana. In September this year I was at Gilwell Park for the annual Wood Badge Reunion. At this gathering there were over 600 men and women from many of the countries that have Scouting.

The Wood Badge training is the ultimate in Boy Scout leader training. Studies have shown that when the leaders have taken part in this training the boys in their units stay in Scouting longer and advance further than the boys in units where the leaders have less training. And if they stay longer we have a better chance to influence their character. You can participate in this training. You can become a Wood Badger. Wood Badge Course NE-IV-III will be held at Hawk Mountain Scout Reservation this fall over three weekends. For the sake of the boys in your unit, heed the kudu call. Sign up today. Come to Gilwell. I'll see you there. [*Herbie Hawk News,* May/June, 1999]

The Forces of Evil Are Loose In the World

The forces of evil are loose in the world. The proof of this is all around us. The recent tragic events in Littleton, Colorado and the reactions to these events are one reminder. Our opinion poll reading political leaders have the rectitude of a weather vane in a tornado. The Boy Scouts are being sued to force us to relinquish our moral principles. The news media celebrates these happenings and happily promotes them. It was summed up nicely for me by Thomas Sowell who recently wrote: "...[I]t is truly galling to have those who have been undermining both morality and parents for years now demand that parents be held legally responsible for the acts of their children."

Yes, the forces of evil are loose in the world but they are not winning no matter what you might read in the papers or see on the television news. For the victories of the forces of good are silent and unreported by the news media. It has been thirty-five years since I last visited Littleton, Colorado. Yet I vividly remember the view as you look West and see the majesty of God's handy work in the vistas of the Rocky Mountains. Many of us also see our children, our grandchildren, and the youth of our community as God's handy work and we are determined to preserve their future. We have determined that we will use Scouting as one of the ways that we will seek to mold the character of our young people. In this we have our silent victories. As an example I point to the recent Eagle Scout Recognition Dinner where we celebrated our most recent Eagle Scouts and listened as they recited their accomplishments and told us about their Eagle projects. For over an hour boy after boy, sixty-four in all, stood before us and told of the stunning tasks that they had undertaken for the betterment of their community. "I painted my neighbor's house." "I built a bridge." "I built a playground." In their matter-of-fact recitations are the sounds of our victory.

It is not about guns or television shows or the lyrics to popular songs. It is about giving our youth a moral compass to steer by. Baden-Powell told us that the one sure hope for the future of the world depended upon youth that lived by the Scout Oath and Law and that believed in themselves, believed in God and believed in their country. It is toward that end that we labor. And we are winning. We can only lose if we despair. The forces of evil that are aligned against us know that the possibility of despair is our only weak point. That is why they have set their propaganda machinery in motion. But we can hear the silent victories. We can see it in the smiling faces of our young people as they raise their hands in the Scout sign and give heartfelt rendition of the

Scout Oath and Law. We can hear it in their laughter. Do not despair. We are winning. And we will win. [*Herbie Hawk News*, July/August, 1999]

Guardian of the Gate

Some of you appear to be standing guard at the gate. Like good guards you are not letting anyone pass who does not have the correct password. When someone appears at the gate who does not have the correct password, you send them away. The treasure that you believe you are guarding is the SACRED ADVANCEMENT REQUIREMENTS. You believe that you must guard the gate to make sure that no boy advances who has not only met the requirements but who has not met the requirements 110%. Your watchword is, "We've gotten soft on the Boy Scout advancement."

The problem is that you have gotten your orders wrong. You are guarding the wrong side of the gate. The treasure is not behind the gate but in front of it. The treasure is the character of the boys in our care. Your duty is not to prevent boys from passing through but to make sure as many boys as possible **do** pass through. Advancement is a method, a tool if you will, that we use in Scouting. It is not an end in itself. The purpose of the advancement system is to build a boy's confidence and self-esteem. A boy learns something new, he is tested in that skill, he is reviewed, and he is given advancement. Whenever possible the test should be a natural part of the unit's program. For example, if the requirement is to cook a meal, the test should come when it's time to eat at a regular unit outing. Remember that we are not authorized to either add to or subtract from any requirement. The review is to be a reflection on a boy's experience in Scouting, not a retest. The advancement recognition must come as soon after the review as possible. Some of you may have heard that advancement recognition can only be received once. I assure you that is not true. Recognition can be made times and as often as possible. Advancement is to be positive reinforcement for a boy's achievements. If done properly it will encourage a boy toward even more advancement and toward greater confidence in himself. So stand clear of the gate. Guard it no more. Gather the boys in your unit and lead them through the gate. The world will be a better place tomorrow. [*Herbie Hawk News,* September/October, 1999]

Basic Unit Finances

I've been conducting an informal survey this summer. I've asked a number of you how you handle finances in your Scout unit. In this survey I've asked two questions. The first is, "How do you take care of the basic financial needs of your unit?" and the second is, "Do you have the boys pay weekly dues?"

I'm happy to report that in answer to the first question many of you are telling me that you use the unit budget plan. On the unit budget plan you list all of the expenses that you expect for the year including the cost of summer camp, re-registration and *Boys' Life.* Then you decide where this money is to come from. Are you going to have money-earning projects? What kind? How many? Are you going to sell popcorn, for example? Are you going to charge dues? How much? Are you going to use the proceeds from these projects to fund summer camp or part of the summer camp fee? Answering all of these questions will help you decide what you want to do. Once you've gone through this process, you'll have a clear financial plan and a picture of what you plan to do in the coming year. I hope that all of you follow this process. It will make life a lot easier for you.

On the subject of weekly dues I got a more divergent opinion. Many of you say that you are charging annual dues for each boy or family. Your reason for this is that it is a "real pain" to collect weekly dues from the boys. The other side of this story is that many of you, while you readily admit that there can be some effort required to collect weekly dues, feel that this is an important part of character building for the boys. Scouting is about inculcating certain values, one of which is, "A Scout is thrifty." By paying weekly dues boys learn to pay their own way as they go. They learn the value of money. For younger boys parents can provide the money based on weekly chores at home. Older boys can earn their weekly dues outside of the home. Thus having the boys pay weekly dues is a tool that we can use to teach boys some of the values we want them to learn. That just might be worth a little trouble and a little "pain in the..." [*Herbie Hawk News,* November/December, 1999]

Turn of the Century

Our Gift of Time

People often ask us why we devote so much time to our Scouting jobs. Some of the people who ask us these questions are close family members. We need to think about how we answer these questions so that we will give the right impression. In my view, we do what we do in Scouting for three reasons:

We believe that a boy should believe in God, believe in his country, and believe in himself. We believe that the best way to accomplish this is through Scouting. We believe the world will be a better place if we make a difference in the life of one boy. We want the values in Scouting to be a vital part of the life of someone we love, perhaps a son, or a grandson. It's fun. The activities are full of fun and adventure. These activities are fun not only for the boys but for the adults involved as well. The people we get to work with are great folks and of like mind with ourselves.

Now in the final analysis, the only thing we can give in this world is our time. Time we give to Scouting is time that we can't devote to our spouses and our families. Time spent in Scouting is time away from our chores at home. Because Scouting is so much fun we sometimes feel guilty about the time we devote to it. But fun is one of the methods of Scouting. If Scouting isn't fun, boys won't be attracted to it. If we could only teach our youth how to enjoy life, it will be the most valuable gift we could give them.

Rather than feel guilty for our service to the brotherhood of Scouting we need to emphasize the first two reasons that we serve. To repeat, these reasons are making the world a better place and the love of a son or grandson. Perhaps if we give these reasons we'll be forgiven the time we devote to this cause. [*Herbie Hawk News,* January/February, 2000]

Be Prepared

The other day I was sitting at the Mall and look down to realize that I had cut my finger. I know what you're thinking, "Another senior moment." Right? Well, without really thinking about it, I reached into my wallet to get the Band-Aid® that I knew would be there. How did I know it would be there? Because in 30 plus years of Scouting I have taught 100's of Scouts to "Be Prepared" in this way. In Scouting our motto is, "Be Prepared." In many, many ways the Scouting programs teaches boys to be prepared. It is perhaps our most important task.

The Cub Scout learns to be prepared to help at a den meeting, to help at a pack meeting, to lead the flag ceremony. He learns to be prepared to deal with an emergency and to help out at home. A Boy Scout learns to be prepared to render first aid. He learns to be prepared for a campout or for summer camp by packing his pack. He learns to be prepared to teach a skill to younger Scouts or to lead a Troop meeting. He learns how to plan the meals and buy the food for an outing. A Venture Crew member learns to be prepared to give leadership to a Crew outing or service project. In these and in many other ways we teach our youth to be prepared.

Do you carry a Band-Aid® in your wallet? The next time you see one there let it remind you that one of our most important jobs is to teach our young people to "Be prepared." [*Herbie Hawk News,* March/April, 2000]

Wood Badge Training

My subject this month is training. I want to be really sure that you get your share. I'd like to be absolutely certain that you get every second of training that you're entitled to. You may readily believe that no organization in the world has more training opportunities for its leaders than Scouting. Your position in Scouting will be made so much easier if you take full advantage of these training opportunities. The extra program dimensions that you will bring back to the youth in your charge will be greatly enhanced if you take all of the training that's available to you.

The most exciting training that's available in Scouting is Wood Badge. The Wood Badge course is advanced leadership training for Pack leaders, Troop leaders, Venture Crew leaders and all District and Council volunteers. It is an experiential training adventure that is second to none. Courses are being held in neighboring Councils in 2000 and a course will be held at Hawk Mountain Scout Reservation in 2001. We especially recommend the course being held in the Susquehanna Council this fall where our good friend Kaylene Trick will be the Scoutmaster. Roger Mory will be the Scoutmaster for our 2001 course. For the sake of your unit and the youth in our community you really must make plans to take the Wood Badge. Your unit should also consider helping unit leaders with the cost of the course.

My challenge to all units is to send at least two people to the Wood Badge. You deserve the very best in training experiences and the course for the Wood Badge is it. Mark your calendar today! Sign up now! Convince your friends to come with you. Two people from each unit—each Pack, Troop and Crew—that's my challenge to you. [*Herbie Hawk News,* May/June, 2000]

Scouting in Our Church

I've just returned from the National Council meeting, held this year in Nashville, Tennessee. A usual highlight of the National meeting is the Duty to God breakfast. And this year was no exception. The keynote speaker was Dr. Joseph Harris, the General Secretary to the General Commission on Methodist Men. Dr. Harris' message was that when we have Scouting in our church we need to see it as a vital part of our ministry. Scouting is a ministry of our church. It is vital because it helps keep the young people connected to the church. We need to keep this in the forefront of our minds. We can't afford to allow a disconnect between the church and Scouting as a ministry.

There are three important ways that Scouting is an important part of our ministry. First of all, Scouting is important as an outreach to the community. Dr. Harris himself came to the church through the example of his Scoutmaster. The young people who join the Scouting programs chartered to our church and their families will often be unchurched. Secondly, Scouting is an opportunity for intergenerational activities that allow older member to be mentors to younger members. Finally, Scouting offers moral training and discipline as a foundation for life. The Scout Oath and Law become a guiding light for our youth. In Scouting our young people learn to live a moral and ethical life. In Scouting Dr. Harris said, "We are about touching the world." His positive and inspiring message in support of Scouting reminds us all to make Scouting a vital part of our ministry to the youth of our community. [*Herbie Hawk News,* July/August, 2000]

Free Yourself to Serve

There is no more uncomfortable feeling than not know what to do or not knowing how to do something. Often in Scouting we encounter a new situation and we don't know how to proceed. We are fettered by our lack of knowledge. We are chained by our lack of training. We are bound by our lack of education. When we lack knowledge and information we feel constrained. Fortunately in Scouting we have resources that can break the chains of ignorance. These resources are the Scouting literature and the Scouting training courses.

Whatever you might be called upon to do in Scouting you can be sure that there is a handbook for that situation or position. Make sure you use the literature of Scouting to break the chains of ignorance. Read the handbooks that are available to free yourself from the constraints that lack of knowledge places upon you.

The same is true of training courses. For every program and for every position there is extensive training available. Fast start training, basic position training and Wood Badge are all part of the training and education offerings. Avail yourself of this training. Take the courses that are offered. The youth of our community are depending on you. Use the training courses that are available to break the chains of ignorance. Free yourself to serve with knowledge and confidence. Break the chains. [*Herbie Hawk News,* November/December, 2000]

"Can't We Just...?"

How often have you heard it, "Can't we just do it this way?"

Everybody today is looking for shortcuts. "Do we have to have that meeting?"

"Can't we just send each other e-mails?"

"Do we have to have advancement in the troop?"

"Do we have to take the Cubs to day camp?"

"Do we have to teach the boys to run their own program?"

"Can't we just do it an easier way?"

"Can't we just...?"

Everybody is looking for the easy way before they've tried anything. To some extent this is understandable. All of us today live busy lives. Our everyday activities are much more active and eventful than our parents ever imagined. We all have more things to do than we'll ever get done. But in seeking shortcuts we often fail to get the job done. In the end we wind up having to do it over. Where we tried to eliminate effort we expended more effort.

In Scouting we have programs. These programs have been designed with the end in mind: character development, citizenship training, and personal fitness for our young people. When we take shortcuts with the Scouting programs, we end up shortcutting our young people. When we eliminate part of the program because we think we see an easier way, we eliminate a part of the program that was designed to keep a boy in Scouting. So the next time someone says, "Can't we just...?", you tell them, "No we can't." Use the full Scouting program. Take full advantage of all that Scouting has to offer. Don't take shortcuts. [*Herbie Hawk News*, January/February, 2001]

Are You Teaching Any Lessons?

We were on a campout recently and someone asked how much a gallon of water weighed. Immediately my grandson answered, "A pint's a pound and there are 8 pints in a gallon, so it must be 8 pounds." The entire saying is, "A pint's a pound the world around except in shot and feathers." My grandmother had been taught this lesson in school as a young girl in about 1880. Now 120 years later a great-great-grandson she never met knows this lesson. Now that's a lesson well learned.

Are you teaching any lessons that will be passed on generation to generation so that 120 years from now people that you'll never meet will still know those lessons?

I believe that you are. We have been teaching the ideals of Scouting through the Oath and Law for over 90 years. If we do our jobs correctly, then the great-great-grandson of one of our Scouts today will be taught these same ideals by the great-grandson of another of our Scouts. Like a pebble thrown into a pond, these lessons ripple through time. Thus 100 years from now they'll say, "On my honor, I will do my best...." We're on the right track. Stay the course. We shall prevail. [*Herbie Hawk News,* March/April, 2001]

Advancement Boards of Review

One of the methods of Scouting is the advancement program. In Boy Scouts part of the advancement system is the Board of Review. Let's review what I have just said. Our <u>aim</u> in Scouting is to develop character, teach citizenship and allow boys to grow in personal fitness. One of the <u>methods</u> we use is the advancement program. All of our methods are designed to increase a boy's desire to stay in

Scouting. We can not achieve our aims if he does not. This was Baden-Powell's original idea. Are you with me so far?

In the advancement program, a boy is tested on requirements often without knowing that he is being tested. When he has been tested, his book is signed or his merit badge card is signed. Once this has happened, he may <u>never</u> be tested on this requirement again. He certainly may not be tested at his board of review. Remember these requirements are part of a method for achieving our aims. They are not an end in themselves. Boards of review may only be held at the unit. This includes boards of review for Eagle Scout. Any of you that may have a different view about this please accept my assurance that you are wrong.

Finally, a board of review must be a positive experience for a boy. It must be a fun. It will be a reflection on his Scouting experience. The board of review should be an encouragement for a boy to remain in Scouting. In no case is a boy to be "grilled" or questioned in any but a friendly and kind manner. For a boy to fail a board of review should be such an extraordinary event that you would feel free to call me and explain it. It fact that is exactly what I would like you to do should this unbelievably, unlikely event occur. I mean that.

If the boards of review in your unit are not fun, reflective, and positive, please be sure that you make them so immediately. If you feel that you are unable to do this, please separate yourself from the advancement program. If you would like my personal advice on how to do *this*, please call me. [*Herbie Hawk News,* May/June, 2001]

How a Scoutmaster Controls and Uses the Advancement

In my last article we discussed the fact that the advancement program is a method of Scouting and not an end in itself. We concluded therefore that the Board of Review experience must be a positive one if we are to make best use of this method. In this article I'd like us to review the three ways that a Scoutmaster controls and uses the advancement program in his Troop.

The first arena is Merit Badges. Merit badges give a boy a chance to explore new areas. The Scoutmaster must approve all Merit Badge cards before the Scout visits the Merit Badge Counselor. This approval process is the Scoutmaster's opportunity to counsel a boy on the kind of Merit Badges that the boy might take. If a boy is not ready for a particular badge then the Scoutmaster can guide him to something else. This guiding must be used judiciously so as to not to discourage a boy.

The second area of interest is rank advancement. The requirements for every rank include a Scoutmaster's conference. This is the Scoutmasters opportunity to counsel a boy not only on his rank advancement but also on all aspects of his development, particularly Scout Spirit. If a boy is not ready for advancement this is the opportunity to counsel him. If a boy needs improvement at this point he must be told very specifically what he needs to do. Remember this is not an opportunity to retest a boy on any of the requirements. This is the time to discuss his Boy Scout Spirit. Even if the Scoutmaster's conference is to have a negative outcome for the boy it should not be a negative experience. If you have counseled correctly, then he will know that you are on his side and are helping him move forward.

The third and most important aspect of the advancement program is recognition. Some people think that recognition can only be given once for each rank advancement but this is simply not true. On the night that a boy passes his

Board of Review an announcement should be made of his achievement. The next week a simple ceremony at a troop meeting will serve to present him with the badge so that he can sew it on his uniform. When I see a Scout who is not wearing the correct rank, I'm lead to believe that you've not recognized him enough for his achievement and made sure he has the badge. A more formal recognition can be made at the quarterly court of honor. Again at the annual court of honor you can recognize him again. Remember the object is to recognize him. Do it often and with due ceremony. [*Herbie Hawk News,* July/August, 2001]

Scout Uniform

President George W. Bush in his recent address to the Jamboree said, "When you join a Scout troop and put on the Boy Scout uniform, you make a statement. Like every uniform, yours is symbol of commitment. It is a sign to all that you believe in high standards, and that you are trying to live up to them every day. As you do that, you bring credit to the Scout uniform and credit to your country. And I want you to know that your country is proud of you."

The uniform is another of our methods in Scouting. It is part of the romance of Scouting. It is a symbol of our ideals and of the outdoor activities of our movement. Since non-scouts often tease boys today, boys are sometimes reluctant to wear their uniform outside of Scouting activities. Nevertheless, within Scouting a boy likes to have a uniform to wear. It gives him a way to show off the badges that he's earned. It gives him pride in his appearance. It helps him feel he belongs to his troop and his patrol and our great world brotherhood; on the same level as other Scouts. In this way the uniform help foster true democracy within the pack and the troop. By dressing alike Scouts show that they are equals. The uniform is also a sign to the Scout and to the world that the wearer is a person who can be trusted; a person who can be counted on to lend a hand when help is needed. Dressed as a Scout a boy will want to act as a Scout.

So please make sure that your unit is properly uniformed. Keep a collection of experienced uniforms to help cut down the cost. Conduct money-earning projects so that the boys can earn part of the money for their uniforms. As the leader make sure that you are properly uniformed. Boys won't wear their uniforms if you don't set the example. Make full use of this Scouting method. [*Herbie Hawk News,* September/October, 2001]

Baden-Powell's Game

Lord Baden-Powell called Scouting a game with a purpose. In the battle to build a boy's character the opposition has, among other things, video games. You, however, have Baden-Powell's game. If you get your boys to play his game to the fullest, you will surely fulfill our mission—to help boys become good citizens of high moral character who are both physically and mentally fit.

B-P's game as we play it today has three versions: Cubs, Scouts and Ventures Crews. Each of these has age appropriate elements. These are—fun, adventure, camping, advancement, uniforms, leadership participation, and the association with adults of good character.

Be sure you let the boy's play all of the game. Don't pick out bits and pieces and thus invent a game of your own. It is B-P's game that we play in Scouting. It is B-P's game that will make us successful. It is B-P's game, Scouting, that will make it possible for us to achieve our goals and fulfill our mission.

Tomorrow will be populated with boys of good character, who are good citizens, both physically and mentally fit, if you play Baden-Powell's game. Play hard. Play to win. Play the whole game. It is B-P's gift to us. It is your gift to tomorrow. Have fun. [*Herbie Hawk News,* November/ December, 2001]

A Scout Is Brave

People are saying that things will never be the same. They are saying that since we have been forced to face the reality of possible enemy attack, our lives have been forever changed.

In many respects this is very true. Our denial of the reality of a possible enemy attack did not make it less likely. As this truth has dawned on people, they have returned to the values that Scouting never left. As our Chief Scout Executive, Roy Williams, has pointed out, "People are sewing American flags on their clothing. Flags that Boy Scouts never took off." People have found religion again. Scouting never strayed. Many American are again showing their patriotism. Flags abound. We were always patriotic. So in this way things have changed. And we hope that they will never be the same again.

Another way that things have changed is through fear. Fear is a major weapon of our enemy. To some extent fear is a good thing. It makes us more aware and alert. What we must not do is give in to fear. If we cower in our homes, afraid to go out, afraid to travel, afraid to go about our business, our enemy will have won. They will have achieved their goals.

We teach our Scouts to be brave. If they are to learn this lesson, they must see us brave. Do not let our enemy win. Live your life to the fullest so that our Scouts can see this and follow in our example. [*Herbie Hawk News,* January/February, 2002]

Multorum Manibus Magnam Levatur Onus

Did you have to take Latin when you were in school? They made us take Latin when I was in the military boarding school. (You know, where Mother sent me as a reward for my good behavior.) I wasn't then but now I'm glad that they did make us. Things sound so much better and so much more memorable when said in Latin. At the moment I'm thinking of a Latin phrase that fits what we need to do to be successful in Scouting

If I tell you to go out and recruit more people, you think that you've heard that before. But if I say, "*Multorum manibus magnam levatur onus.*" ("Many hands make labors light.") Well, doesn't that sound more dignified? Isn't that so much more elegant when you say it in Latin? Whatever your Scouting job, you need to get more people involved. You need to get more help. And people are just waiting for you to ask them. As one ADC told me recently, there are many people, "...moving around the edge of the ballroom but have never really danced." They're just waiting for you to ask them to "dance." They want to help but they don't know how. You've got to ask them. You've got to show them how to help. Remember. *Multorum manibus magnam levatur onus.* ("Many hands make labors light.") [*Herbie Hawk News,* March/April, 2002]

Unpublished Stories

Bryan's Prayer

We were on a fall campout. We camped starting on Friday night at French Creek State Park. The weather had been chilly and rainy all weekend. We got up Sunday morning. The program Sunday morning was to have breakfast and then break camp. A first year Scout, Bryan, was asked to say Grace. This is Bryan's prayer.

> *Lord, thank you for the food we are about to eat.*
> *Thank you for keeping us safe.*
> *And thank you for the fun we had this weekend.*
>
> *Amen*

I had the privilege on October 22, 2006 to go to Bryan Focht's Eagle Court of Honor

Life is Good

As I ride along in the fall afternoon, I celebrate life. Life is good. There are of course moments but they pass. The integral is that life is fun and life is wonderful. This is what we have to teach our Scouts. B-P said it best when he said, "A Scout is cheerful."

I Feel Lucky

You will understand that I am no longer a young man

when I tell you that I've been taking Boy Scouts to a week of summer camp since 1970. One very recent summer I was walking up the hill to our camp site with Mark, an eleven year old first year camper. I felt the need to stop and take a rest.

"Let's stop for a rest," I said. "Fifty years from now when you're my age, you'll understand the need to stop and take a rest."

"Well, Mr. Daley, I'm sure you feel lucky" Mark informed me, "at your age to be as active as you are." I had to admit, I did.

Dr. Avery Post

In one issue [*Herbie Hawk News*, October, 1986. I left out the article I wrote for this issue because after 20 years I'm sure the information is dated.] there was a story about the presentation of the God and Service Award at the Good Shepard U.C.C. Church in Boyertown, PA, to Dr. Avery Post who at the time was the President of the United Church of Christ. The presentation was made by Paul Hafer (a past Council President), Gene Gable (District Camping Chairman and Chartered Organization Representative), Gene Druckenmiller (a past Council Commissioner), Gerry White (Advisory Board member), David Sharp (Scout Executive) and me. We were there representing the National United Church of Christ Association of Scouters (NUCCAS) which at the time had been newly formed largely by the efforts of Paul Hafer. Paul Hafer was a past Council President of the Hawk Mountain Council. He was also a founder and the force behind the founding of NUCCAS. He was on the National Relationships Committee for many years and originated the term "Chartered Partner." He was awarded the Silver Beaver, Silver Antelope and the Silver Buffalo.

At a reception just prior to the service where the presentation was made Dr. Post related to us how he had come to the church. As a youth his family had been unchurched. The Scout Troop he joined was chartered to a Roman Catholic Church. In the troop were boys who belonged to the U.C.C. Church and he started going to church with them. In time he heard a calling to the ministry and rose to become the president of a major protestant denomination. He believed that his path was started in Scouting. This is something to keep in mind when you take your Scouts to church on Scout Sunday or when you're on a campout. You never know where the path will lead.

POEMS

The Boy Scout's Mother Asked

[*Herbie Hawk News*, October, 1991 I have read this poem
at over 500 Eagle Scout presentations.]

"Where has my little baby gone?"
The Cub Scout's Mother asked,
"He went by here awhile ago.
Did you not see him pass?"

He'd gone to be a Tiger Cub
And then a Wolf was he.
He learned to carve the pinewood car,
And sing the songs with glee.

And after that he was a Bear,
And then a Webelo Scout.
He learned the Boy Scout Oath and Law,
And fun in full amount.

Crossed over to be a Boy Scout,
And shown what kindness meant.
His best is what he'd have to be,
Everywhere he went.

"Where has my baby boy gone?"
The Boy Scout's Mother asked,
"He went by here awhile ago.
Did you not see him pass?"

To hike the trails and pitch a tent,
To swim the lakes and streams,
To kindle a fire under the stars,
These were his every day dreams.

Down the long trail to Eagle,
He smilingly went his way.
The many adventures that he had,
Shaped the man we see today.

Learned to be a citizen,
A helping hand to lend.
He learned what cheerful service means,
And how to be a friend.

"Where has my baby boy gone?"
The Boy Scout's Mother asked,
"He went to be a Boy Scout,
And he grew to be a man."

ME? A SCOUT?

by Robert E. Besecker [*Herbie Hawk,* October, 1995]
Bob Besecker, then our Assistant Council Commissioner
for Operation Saturation and now a professional Scouter,
always my good friend, agreed to let me share this with you.

Me? A Scout?
That's what I want to be.
A shirt of orange, a Tiger Cub,
Just Mom and Dad and me.

Me? A Scout?
I'm a 2nd grader now.
I'll work real hard to be a Wolf,
If you'll just show me how.

Cub Scouting's fun! I'm now a Bear.
A pocketknife to show!
Time to make my pinewood car,
Dad'll help, I know.

Me? A Scout? A Webelos Scout,
And all my best friends too!
Learning 'bout so many things,
And so many things to do.

Now it's time to cross the bridge,
It should be quite a night.
It's really hard for me to think,
Me? The Arrow of Light!

Me? A Scout? A Boy Scout.
So many skills to learn.
Tenderfoot, Second Class, First Class,
So many ranks to earn.

I'll work real hard through Star and Life,
and work in Cheerful Service too.
Seems so long since I was Cubbing,
When everything was new.

Me? A Scout? An Eagle Scout!
I'm surely flyin' high.
A Scout is what I'll always be,
The Spirit shall not die.

The Eagle Uniform

By Admiral Henry "Hank" Childs At the military
boarding school where my parents sent me as a reward for
my good behavior, we were required to memorize a poem by

Eustace S. Glascock, McDonogh School Class of 1879, called "The McDonogh Uniform." A classmate of mine, sent to the military school for the same reason, Admiral Henry "Hank" Childs, has adapted this poem for Scouting by changing only four of the words. [*Herbie Hawk News*, November, 1994]

> An Eagle suit for your son to wear?
> Ah! Madam, they're not for sale.
> And he who dons must never doff—
> As a nun who takes the veil.
>
> 'Tis a matter of years to make the fit,
> And the cloth is rich and rare,
> With "Be Prepared" running through warp and woof,
> And woven with scrupulous care.
>
> With labor and patience, with wisdom and love,
> Every thread is drawn to its place.
> 'Tis dyed in the colors of honor and truth,
> With industry's infinite grace.
>
> The dirt and grime of strife and toil
> Only brighten its marvelous hue;
> But the shiftless shame of an idle life
> Will rot it through and through.
>
> Measures we take, but not with a tape—
> For we tailor to fit a man's soul
> With a garment to wear, thro' life's arduous race
> And bring him in safe at the goal.
>
> Our trade-mark is woven into every suit,
> 'Tis a vow that each wearer must make.
> How low or how high in the world he may be:
> "We Give Something More Than We Take."

Yet we have no weaver of magical skill,
Our tailor's no Fairyland elf.
We've merely discovered that to wear such a suit
The wearer must make it himself.

Back Behind the Tooth of Time

Have you been to Philmont? Have your Scouts been to Philmont? Philmont is the ultimate fulfillment of the adventure we promise a boy when he joins Scouting. I was at Philmont in June [1998] and I was moved to write this poem. All of the things enumerated in this poem actually happened and on that day. [*Herbie Hawk News*, September/October, 1998]

Back Behind the Tooth of Time
(Sunday, June 7, 1998)

Back Behind the Tooth of Time
A gentle peace was this day mine.
Early saw we elk and calf
Flushed from out their morning bath.
Black bear ambled to the wood.
Beaver swam the best he could.
Horses with the Philmont brand,
Called out to us as we passed.
Quail quaked in the grass alone.
Buffalo refused to roam.
Squirrel scampered down the path.
Mountain Blue birds flew all day.
Bull snake catching sunny rays
Indignantly slithered away.
Just another Philmont day!

Chanced upon a magpie meeting.
Spoke they all in solemn greeting.

Antelope to his abode
Raced passed us down the road.
Thistle, deadly prickly poppy
Flowered gaily on the verge.
Aspen sparkling in the breeze.
Cottonwood trees snowing seeds.
Indian Paintbrush painted
Grasslands carpeted for cattle.
Mule deer listening in the dew
Like campfires remembered, too,
Sunset blazed in fire-like hue
From mountain tops far away.
Just another Philmont day!

2978467

Made in the USA